CREATING
COTTAGE
STYLE

CREATING COTTAGE STYLE

KATHERINE SORRELL

STYLISH IDEAS AND STEP-BY-STEP PROJECTS

RYLAND
PETERS
& SMALL
LONDON NEW YORK

SENIOR DESIGNER Sally Powell

DESIGNER Sarah Fraser

EDITOR Miriam Hyslop

PICTURE RESEARCH Emily Westlake

PRODUCTION Sheila Smith

ART DIRECTOR Gabriella Le Grazie

PUBLISHING DIRECTOR Alison Starling

First published in the United States in 2005
by Ryland Peters & Small, Inc.
519 Broadway
5th Floor
New York, NY 10012
www.rylandpeters.com

Text © Katherine Sorrell 2005
The additional credits on page 112
constitute part of this copyright page.
Design and photographs ©
Ryland Peters & Small 2005

10 9 8 7 6 5 4 3 2 1

ISBN (Paperback) 1 84172 942 6
ISBN (Hardcover) 1 84597 065 9

Printed and bound in China

Library of Congress Cataloging-in-Publication Data

Sorrell, Katherine.
  Creating cottage style : stylish ideas and step-by-step
projects /
Katherine sorrell.– 1st ed.
      p. cm.
  Includes index.
  ISBN 1-84172-942-6
  1. Handicraft. 2. Cottages–Decoration. 3. Decoration
and ornament,
Rustic. I. Title.
  TT157.S632 2005
  747–dc22

                          2005012217

introduction

Whether you are about to embark on a head-to-toe makeover of your home or simply want to freshen up a room or two, this book aims to help with both inspirational and practical ideas for introducing country style. In every chapter there are quick tips and more detailed projects, some of them instant and inexpensive, others a little more ambitious. If you are good with your hands and have a little time to spare, you will find them all satisfying to make and attractive to live with.

Cottage style is a relaxed and easy-going aesthetic that is more about emotion—how your environment makes you feel—than sticking rigidly to a particular set of rules. So use this book as a guide, taking the elements to which you are drawn and adapting them to your home and your way of life. The result will be a look that is as timelessly appealing as it is unique to you.

cottage

Why decorate in cottage style? Most people's answer would be because it suits not only their home, but also their way of life, for whether you live in an idyllic rural setting, by the coast, or in the middle of a city, there is something tremendously appealing about an interior that is warm and welcoming, individual and eclectic—a look that is simple, but that has its own charming sophistication. It is the very opposite of the grand, stuffy, keep-up-with-the-Joneses type of decorating where order, symmetry, and neatness are paramount and you can't put a book down without feeling that you've made a mess. Instead, cottage style allows you to mix old and new with hand-me-downs and junk-store finds, and to combine colors, patterns, textures, fabrics, and accessories with gusto and laidback informality. This is a look that reflects traditional styles, the beauty of the natural world, and ultimately, your own personal sense of surroundings, and that is both practical and pleasurable.

style

TOP ROW, LEFT TO RIGHT *A large-scale pattern of twining flowers in muted colors is typically English, and provides a lovely backdrop to an eclectic selection of furniture. Natural materials such as stone, wood, and wicker are key elements of this style. For a highly feminine bedroom, choose floral walls teamed with a floral quilt and bunches of casually arranged fresh flowers.*

BOTTOM ROW, LEFT TO RIGHT *These tongue-and-groove cupboards are new, but fit perfectly with the traditional spindle-back armchair and the rise-and-fall lamp. Heavy curtains and a comfortable sofa upholstered in a wide check bring warmth and coziness to this room. For the traditional look of a country bathroom, patterned ceramics and simple accessories, such as this shell-shaped soap dish, are ideal.*

English style

If you dream of a thatched cottage with roses around the door, chickens in the backyard, and a cake baking in the range, then English style is for you. Pretty as a picture and as unpretentious as it comes, it is comfortable without being lavish, charming without being fussy, and idiosyncratic without being eccentric (well, not too eccentric, anyway). It is a look that is never self-consciously fashionable, but never quite out of fashion, either. It is the look that evokes the England of cricket on the village green, strawberries and cream for tea, new-mown hay, and church bells on a summer's evening. Harmonious and restful, English country interiors employ natural materials, honest furniture, pretty fabrics, and a confident mix of colors, patterns, and textures to create a rural retreat that instinctively appeals to all the senses.

American style

At the root of the American country style is a cheerful comfortableness that reflects the early settlers' spirit of hard work, practicality, and self-sufficiency. Sturdy, unembellished furnishings are mixed with bright and simple folk art and crafts—reminiscent of the familiar decorations of the settlers' varied European homelands. With function and comfort paramount, there are a few essential ingredients, some or all of which are usually found in every American country-style home: paneled walls, a spindle-backed rocking chair, punched tinware, naïve paintings of people and farmyard animals, rag rugs, and of course a boldly patterned patchwork quilt.

As a background, colors are predominantly cream and buttermilk, soft blue, verdigris, gray, and earthy brown, plus an evocative "barn red" made using oxides from the soil, in various shades from brown to russet. Colorful but down-to-earth fabrics complete the picture, creating a look that has survived centuries to inspire generations with its dignified, unfussy good looks.

TOP ROW, LEFT TO RIGHT *The functional appearance of this bathroom is softened by the bright, patterned rug and the Shaker-style chair in the corner. Cozy seating, colorful fabrics, a rag rug, and naïve decorations—this comfortable sitting room has all the right ingredients. There's no mistaking the distinctive American patchwork quilt, here teamed with twin pencil-post beds, gingham curtains, and a Shaker peg rail. Bold colors and traditional furnishings, including a pair of rockers, a spool daybed, a dough box, and a pie safe, give this sitting room a timeless appeal.*

BOTTOM, LEFT *Simplicity is the key to this room, which is decorated with unfussy colors and natural materials.*

BOTTOM, FAR LEFT *The painted decoration is original to this renovated 1857 Texas ranch. Bold colors, such as this gorgeous deep turquoise, are common in American country homes.*

TOP ROW, LEFT *The mix of furniture styles here creates an eclectic look that is nevertheless coherent and easy on the eye, aided by the pale and pretty color scheme.*

TOP ROW, CENTER AND RIGHT *This simple white room, with its old beams and planked walls, could be almost anywhere and date from any time, but the toile de Jouy pillows add instant French style.*

BOTTOM, LEFT *Old-fashioned simplicity has enduring appeal, and this bathroom is no exception. Although as a whole it is quite spartan, there is generosity in the deep roll-top bathtub and a quirky luxury in the gilt-framed painting of a woman bathing.*

BOTTOM, RIGHT *This carved hutch is a lovely example of French design: elegant, pretty, and practical all at the same time.*

French style

French style is, undeniably, the most chic and sophisticated of all the country styles, and yet it can easily be adapted to any home, from a humble farmhouse to an imposing chateau. Despite being a mix of antique and new furnishings, flea-market finds, and objets d'art, this is a look that is effortlessly harmonious and cohesive, the imaginative mix of pieces being unified by their effortless prettiness. In the scroll of an arm, the curve of a chandelier, the carving of a frieze, the painted decoration of a jug, there is always an uncontrived elegance and lightness of touch. Classic Louis-style furniture is a good starting point for this look, combined with more rustic pieces such as dressers, armoires, and side tables. Colors are pale and interesting, including cream, dove gray, taupe, stone, mid-blue, and lemon yellow, with fabric including either exuberant Provençal prints or more sophisticated monochrome toile de Jouy.

Scandinavian style

Scandinavian cottage style is marked by its combination of simple charm with understated grandeur, warmth, and unpretentiousness with elegance and an uncluttered sense of space and light. In the typical Scandinavian country interior, an appreciation of traditional craft skills such as carving, painting, and weaving combines with a use of natural materials and lively colors to create an interior that is both honest and original. Perhaps the best-known individual Scandinavian style, however, emerged in the late 18th century under King Gustav III of Sweden: known as Gustavian style, it is a blend of strict neo-classicism and rococo gaiety with a gentle, accessible individuality, using subtle pale colors, gilding, mirrors, delicate wooden furniture, glass chandeliers, and floral swags. Neither prescriptively urban nor rural, it is a look that transcends place, class, and time, as pretty and practical in a modest home as in a palace, and as distinctive and delightful as it was 250 years ago.

ABOVE, FAR LEFT AND LEFT *An uncluttered airiness makes this style distinctive, while pale colors and patterned textiles bring softness and comfort.*

ABOVE, CENTER *White-painted floorboards are clean and fresh and reflect light beautifully.*

ABOVE, RIGHT *Checked fabric in a primary color is typically Scandinavian.*

ABOVE, FAR RIGHT *This simple blue runner is Swedish and dates back to the 1930s, setting the scene for a timeless Scandinavian bedroom.*

BELOW *A sense of calm prevails here, thanks to a strictly limited color palette, plain furnishings, and minimal accessories.*

RIGHT *This cozy room features a pleasant combination of wood-paneled walls, a frivolous chandelier, and quality furniture with squashy upholstery.*

cottage

Colorful or neutral, pretty or plain, the timeless, enduring appeal of country-cottage style—whether American or European—extends throughout the house. From the entrance hall to the back door, the attic to the basement, you can add the relaxed charm of country style to every corner. In the living room, you can create an informal space that is welcoming, cozy, and convivial, while the bedroom will be softly comfortable, calm, and relaxing. The country-style bathroom is as functional as you need it to be, while also being nurturing and indulgent; in the dining room, the style is warm and inviting, and in the kitchen, the heart of every country home, it comes into its own as a functional, appealing focal point for family life.

rooms

Warm and welcoming, relaxing and inviting, the cottage-style living room is a cozy, informal space in which to put one's feet up in front of a roaring fire. The key elements are soft colors, a harmonious mix of gentle patterns, and a subtle blend of appealing textures. Furniture is unfussy: a squashy sofa is a must, covered with a scattering of pretty cushions

living rooms

and perhaps a cozy throw or two, coordinating with gathered curtains or plain blinds. On the floor might be wooden boards with ethnic rugs, a tactile carpet, or nubbly natural matting. Planked or paneled doors complement walls covered in either tongue and groove, flat-finish latex, or delicate wallpaper, while finishing touches might include paintings and prints, mirrors, collections of china or wooden objects, photographs, and, of course, vases of fresh flowers.

CLOCKWISE FROM CENTER *Sew a deep hem along the long edge of a pretty tea towel and thread it over a slender pole for an informal (and inexpensive) window treatment. The gentle colors and simple pattern of this woven carpet make it a lovely choice. Make cozy chair cushions from square fabric remnants (it doesn't matter if they don't match exactly), sewing a pair of long ties to each corner to attach them easily. A mix of informal patterns really helps to create the look; adding pillows and throws to a comfortable sofa is a good way to start. A series of prints looks fantastic when framed identically and hung in a neat row. If you choose a monochrome color palette, as in this all-white living room, introduce a variety of textures for interest and appeal.*

colors & textures

A cottage-style living room could be relatively plain, using cool, calm, and neutral colors that don't draw attention to themselves, or it could be rich and intense, filled with bold shades that bring warmth and vibrancy. Texture, too, is highly important, as with texture comes sensuous appeal and an easy sense of comfort.

Start by considering your walls and floor, the largest surfaces in the room and therefore the areas that will have the biggest and most immediate impact. For this look, uneven and imperfect finishes are fine, perhaps even desirable. Walls could be bare brick or plaster, wood paneling, or tongue and groove, or you may prefer patterned wallpaper. With painted walls, you could add decorative borders of paper or stenciling, or try your hand at a broken paint effect such as stippling, sponging, or ragging. On the floor, wall-to-wall carpets are warm and cozy, while natural floor coverings such as jute, sisal, or coir have a suitably rustic appeal. Brick, stone, tiles, or wooden boards are all attractive and an effective

OPPOSITE, TOP LEFT *In a neutral scheme such as this, textural contrasts provide a great deal of the interest, and despite its plain colors and relative austerity, this living room is very appealing. There's a nice balance of hard and soft surfaces, with the carved detailing of the cupboard doors adding a pretty finishing touch.*

OPPOSITE, TOP RIGHT *Natural color schemes can be very calm and serene. This light-filled room has a quiet charm and looks very comfortable.*

OPPOSITE, BELOW *Pale colors predominate in this pretty room, which has a lovely range of natural materials that make for appealing textural contrasts. The terracotta-tiled floor has a gorgeous warmth that is emphasized by its juxtaposition with off-white latex surfaces and pillows in subtle shades.*

The dark paintings make an intriguing contrast.

RIGHT *This boldly patterned wallpaper makes an eye-catching backdrop in this rather grand country living room. Solid colors are used elsewhere, picking up the colors of the paper, along with natural wood and metal.*

BELOW *If you choose neutral walls and floors, you can inject dashes of color and texture in the form of painted-wood furniture—the more distressed, the better. A hutch might not seem an obvious item to place in the corner of a living room, but here it provides a perfect way of displaying a collection of simple, rustic pottery. The chest makes a great informal coffee table.*

LEFT *This simple scene shows just how effective a pleasing mix of textures can be.*

ABOVE *You can't beat the warmth of a wall painted in earthy reddish-brown, a natural color that is ideally suited to a cottage interior. Here, it is highlighted effectively by simple, pure white upholstery.*

RIGHT *The indigo/turquoise paint on these walls has been sponged on for a dramatically mottled effect and has a look that is both informal and inviting. Vivid colors have been added in the form of the bolsters and throw on the sofa and the bold paintings. The overall look is intense and personal, but not overwhelming.*

base for this look, but you will undoubtedly want to soften them with an assortment of rugs.

These key areas provide you with the textural and color backbone of your scheme. So, for example, pale and neutral schemes might involve the gray patina of stone, limewashed wood, cream-painted walls, and unbleached cotton, while brighter schemes may use chintzey wallpaper and fabric, deep paint colors, and polished, dark wood.

Use furniture, textiles, and accessories to enhance your basic scheme. For an elegant look, choose plain colors that harmonize and complement so that the whole room is based around a variation of just one or two shades; for a more eclectic, dynamic look, a varied range of colors and patterns can be exciting. Textural contrasts arise quite naturally—by putting a wicker basket on a wooden floor next to a velvet-covered armchair, for example—but there's no harm in taking some time to think about textures with a little extra care to make sure the overall feel of the room is truly inspiring and inviting.

PROJECT 1

display frame

Frames are not especially difficult to make, though you will need the right tools and a little time and patience, as accurate measuring, sawing, and mitering are vital. This simple box frame is ideal for displaying a collection of small treasures, perhaps pressed leaves or flowers, shells, or feathers, for example. If the soft gilt finish doesn't suit your room scheme, simply give the box a coat of ordinary latex paint in a suitable color.

MATERIALS & EQUIPMENT

½ x 1 inch (12.5 x 25 mm) softwood, 32 inches (800 mm) length, for front

1½ x 5 inches (38 x 125 mm) softwood, 32 inches (800 mm) length, for sides

masonite, approximately 5 x 5 inches (125 x 125 mm), for backing (cut to fit)

picture glass, cut to fit

tenon saw • miter box • wood glue

4 miter clamps or framing clamps

4 corrugated fasteners

hammer • brads • C-clamps

4 metal framing clips

2 ring and eye sets

picture wire

red ocher latex • gilt cream

broad artist's brush

medium sandpaper • 2 soft cloths

1 Use a miter box and tenon saw to cut the narrower softwood into four equal 6 inch (150 mm) lengths, mitering the corners at 45°. Glue the pieces together at the corners to form the flat front of the frame. Clamp until the glue has dried and reinforce the joints with corrugated fasteners before removing the clamps (see page 104).

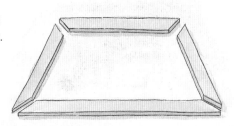

2 Using the miter box and tenon saw, cut the 1½ x 5 inch (38 x 125 mm) softwood into four equal lengths of 6 inches (150 mm), mitering the corners at 45°. These lengths fit together to form a deep box that is attached to the back of the flat frame.

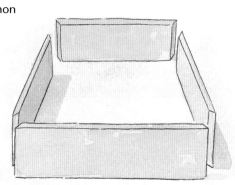

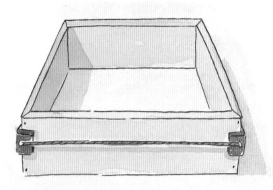

3 Glue the four sides of the box together and clamp the corners until the glue has bonded.

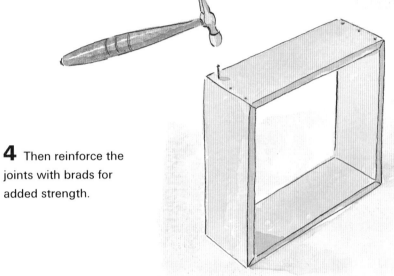

4 Then reinforce the joints with brads for added strength.

STEPS TO PAINT

5 Apply a base coat of red ocher latex to the front, sides, and inside edges of the box.

6 When dry, roughen the surface with medium sandpaper.

7 Apply the gilt cream to the roughened surface, rubbing it in well with a soft cloth so that some of the red shows through.

8 When dry, polish to give a shiny finish.

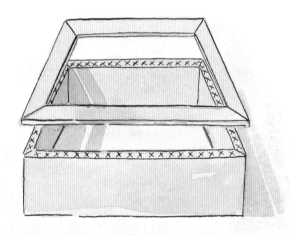

9 Glue the flat frame front onto the deep box and clamp until bonded.

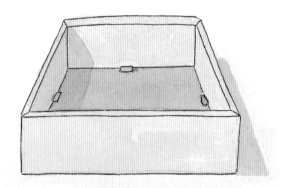

10 Cut the board to fit and have a glazier cut the picture glass. Secure with metal framing clips and attach picture wire to hang the frame.

fabrics

OPPOSITE, TOP LEFT AND RIGHT *When combining patterns, choose colors that either match or are from the same family (pale blues with dark blues, for example). Florals are easier to mix with stripes and checks than with other florals.*

OPPOSITE, CENTER LEFT *A sofa upholstered in a bold floral fabric is always eye-catching. Here, it is teamed with a white-painted floor and another sofa in plain chocolate, so the effect is pretty but laid back and modern.*

OPPOSITE, CENTER RIGHT *The plain upholstery of this sofa is an easy backdrop on which to throw an assortment of cushions. Hung from a metal pole, the gathered curtain is quietly complementary.*

BOTTOM ROW, FROM LEFT TO RIGHT *To jazz up a plain wooden chair, it's easy to make a floral chair pad, adding long ties for a pretty, country effect. These checked cushions are large and soft, and look highly inviting to sink into. To make a set of informal cushion covers, simply sew plain squares of felt together, using blanket stitch around the edges. More or less any sofa can be disguised with a large throw and piles of pillows.*

Fabrics play a key part in setting the scene for a country-style living room, bringing warmth, softness, and a cozy sense of comfort, as well as a variety of appealing colors, patterns, and textures. In general, it's best not to try too hard to coordinate fabrics, as a lived-in, unstudied mix will give a nicely informal effect—and if they appear gently worn, so much the better.

Your top priority, generally, will be to choose curtains, sofa covers and cushions, though you may also have chair covers, bolsters, tablecloths, throws, blinds, lampshades, and wall hangings to consider, too. Try to maintain a balance between fashionably unfussy, streamlined soft furnishings and the frilly prettiness that is typical of cottage style. Curtains, for example, could be generously gathered, perhaps with trimmed edgings or contrasting borders; upholstery should be straightforwardly shaped, with skirts and buttoning but no unnecessary flounces; and slipcovers or large throws can do wonders to transform tired or unsuitable furniture.

Cotton (plain and twilled), canvas, muslin, linen, and wool are all good basic fabrics; for extra interest you might consider felt, denim,

FAR RIGHT *A combination of sunny yellow and deep crimson makes this a very inviting corner. The velvet cushions are really cozy and tactile.*

RIGHT *This checked blind has a pleasantly informal feel that complements the soft cushions on the seat below.*

BELOW *Patchwork has an eternal, informal appeal. Here a quilt has been used as a cover for a sofa that's piled high with cushions in various fabrics, colors, and patterns.*

velvet, silk, or mohair—how heavy, hard-wearing, and dirt-resistant the fabric needs to be will obviously depend on what you're using it for. Solid colors are a good starting point, but for many people this look is dramatically enhanced by introducing patterns. You might consider tweed, for example, with its interesting weave and subtly intermixed colors, or plaid for a bright, warming effect. Gingham, narrow stripes, or tiny dots are subtle yet interesting, while chintz, paisley, tapestry, windowpane checks, broad stripes, and floral or geometric patterns will make more of a statement. You don't have to stick rigidly to a fabric's intended or original use—a lightweight rug might be ideal to throw over the back of a sofa, for example, or a wool blanket to gather up as a warm, thick curtain, while fabric remnants can be gathered together and made into a length of patchwork, the ultimate country fabric, which could be used for anything from an armchair cover to a windowseat cushion.

PROJECT 2
linen pillow cover

Freshen up a tired sofa or armchair with a new pillow or two in a style that is elegant yet unpretentious. This cover is very easy to make—two squares of linen with pairs of ties on each side sandwich an inner cover made from a contrasting fabric. It looks charming in these beige and red stripes, but any relatively lightweight fabric could be used, as long as you make sure the inner cover complements the outer one effectively.

MATERIALS & EQUIPMENT

24 inches (60 cm) beige striped linen fabric, 45 inches (115 cm) wide

20 inches (50 cm) red striped cotton fabric, 45 inches (115 cm) wide

192 inches (500 cm) cotton tape in brown, 1 inch (2.5 cm) wide

192 inches (500 cm) cotton tape in cream, ½ inch (1 cm) wide

18 inch (45 cm) square pillow form

1 For the outer pillow, cut out two pieces of fabric from the striped linen, each 22 inches (55 cm) square. Make sure the stripes run parallel with two of the sides.

2 Take one of the pieces and fold in ¼ inch (5 mm) all around, overlapping the corners. Then fold in ¾ inch (2 cm) and press, making sure the stripes match on the wrong side of the fabric. Repeat for the other piece.

3 To make the ties, place the narrow cream tape in the middle of the brown tape and machine-stitch as close to the edges of the narrow tape as possible to secure together. Cut into 16 strips of 12 inches (30 cm) lengths and press.

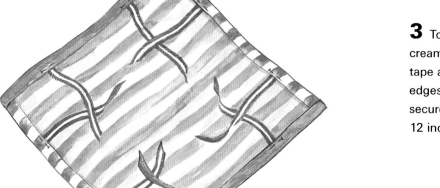

4 Lay one of the squares wrong side up and tuck one length of tape right side up 5 inches (13 cm) from each corner, under the pressed edge. Pin ties in place.

5 To secure the ties to the pillow cover, machine stitch as close as possible to the inner edge of the turned-in seam, sewing across each of the ties. Make sure the ties are straight.

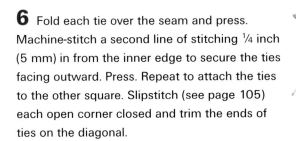

6 Fold each tie over the seam and press. Machine-stitch a second line of stitching ¼ inch (5 mm) in from the inner edge to secure the ties facing outward. Press. Repeat to attach the ties to the other square. Slipstitch (see page 105) each open corner closed and trim the ends of ties on the diagonal.

7 To make the inner pillow, cut out two pieces from the red striped cotton, each 19 inches (48 cm) square. Lay the squares right sides together. Pin, baste, and machine-stitch a seam line ½ inch (1 cm) in from the outside edge around three sides.

8 Turn the cover right side out and press. Insert the pillow form and slip-stitch the opening to a neat close.

9 Place the inner pillow in the middle of one outer panel (wrong side up), then put the other panel over it (wrong side down) and tie up to close.

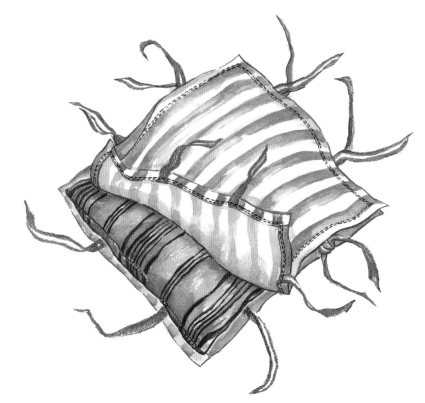

LEFT *The focal point of this living room is undoubtedly the fireplace, with its imposing portrait above and pair of urns arranged symmetrically on the mantelpiece. The huge wicker basket alongside is used for storing logs, but is also a decorative piece in itself.*

BELOW, LEFT *Use herbs and foliage rather than formal cut flowers to scent and color a room. And think laterally about containers—a metal pitcher, glass milk bottle, or painted ceramic pot are all just as pretty as a "proper" vase.*

BELOW, CENTER *Bowls of snipped herbs and flower petals add a colorful, fragrant touch.*

BELOW, RIGHT *Chopped logs can be a feature in their own right, and this beautifully patterned bark is certainly worth including as a textural contrast—it's almost a shame to burn them.*

OPPOSITE *The old glass in this overmantel mirror simply adds to its attraction, and it fits well into this homey living room, where old fire irons are propped against the fireplace and stenciled decorations have been used to enhance the walls above the built-in cupboards.*

finishing touches

Country-cottage style can be plain and simple, but it is never stark or severe, and even just a few carefully chosen finishing touches can transform an uninviting room into one that is warm and comfortable, informal and welcoming.

The fireplace is often the focal point of a living room, and a log basket or coal scuttle will possibly be a necessity rather than an accessory. Add a set of old-fashioned tools propped casually alongside, and you have a look that is timeless and enduring, found in rural properties from the tiniest of cottages to the grandest manor house. And above the mantelpiece it is traditional to hang or prop either a large, gilded mirror or a painting. If you have room on top of the fireplace you might want to arrange a few accessories, such as candlesticks, vases, or family photographs. In fact, photographs can

BELOW, LEFT *The plain shades of small table lamps can easily be embellished with ribbons, braid, buttons, or feathers. Alternatively, you could stencil or paint on a motif.*

BELOW, RIGHT *Books really do furnish a room, and there's nothing to beat the whimsical charm of a set of old Penguin paperbacks.*

OPPOSITE, ABOVE *A small collection of glassware, some robust, some more refined, is displayed to advantage on a table by a window, where the light emphasizes the delicacy of the material. The display of foliage is also highly striking.*

OPPOSITE, BELOW, FROM LEFT TO RIGHT *Casual arrangements of flowers—perhaps hand-picked from your garden—*

look very sweet displayed in unusual containers, such as an old preserving jar. This wooden candle box is a useful storage piece but also looks delightful and is the sort of accessory that adds authenticity to any cottage-style scheme. Decorations need not be expensive—these hand-pressed leaves make an appealing feature, yet cost nothing.

be gathered on any available surface, along with glassware and ceramics (floral-printed, spongeware, or blue-and-white china are all charming) or wicker baskets of all shapes and sizes—useful for storage as well as attractive in themselves.

Rows of old hardback books, or other classics with their distinctive graphic covers, add a lived-in feel, while on the walls you could hang framed needlepoint samplers, equestrian prints, or woodblock illustrations, as well as drawings and paintings.

Display collections on shelves or windowledges and, if you are lucky enough to own one, you might want to place a family heirloom, such as a wooden rocking horse, a hand-made dollhouse, or a grandfather clock in a convenient spot. Position a selection of charming lamps on side tables or shelves around the room—you could, perhaps, enhance their shades with personal touches such as a stenciled motif or a trim made from ribbon, feathers, or buttons. Finally, for a real scent of the countryside, use boxes and bowls to hold pine cones and potpourri, and arrange cut flowers, foliage, and herbs informally in simple containers such as Mason jars or enamel pitchers.

PROJECT 3

pumpkin display

Hollowed-out pumpkins lit by candles placed inside make a wonderful Halloween display, their crudely carved faces once believed to ward off evil spirits. As an alternative fall display, perhaps to be used as a table centerpiece, pumpkins make perfect natural containers for foliage, berries, and candles. This project is very quick to complete and needs hardly any equipment or materials—you could quite easily use a selection of fruit and leaves snipped from your own garden.

MATERIALS & EQUIPMENT

pumpkin, approximately 7 x 8½ inches (18 x 22 cm) diameter

1 block floral foam, 3 x 4½ x 3 inches (8 x 11 x 8 cm)

3 sprigs rosehips (*Rosa*)

5 sprigs blackberries (*Rubus fruticosus*)

5 sprigs guelder rose (*Viburnum opulus*)

8 sprigs fruiting ivy (*Hedera*)

3 purple beeswax candles, 10 x 1 inches (25 x 2.5 cm) diameter

knife • spoon • medium-gauge florist's wire • wire cutters

tape • florist's scissors

1 Using a sharp knife, cut out a neat square in the top of the pumpkin, measuring 3¼ x 3¼ inches (8.5 x 8.5 cm). Lift off the top and then use a spoon to scoop out the flesh inside to a depth of about 4¾ inches (12 cm).

2 Thoroughly soak the block of floral foam in water, then insert it snugly into the pumpkin, pushing it down so that the top edge is flush with the surface of the pumpkin.

3 Cut six pieces of medium-gauge florist's wire approximately 4 inches (10 cm) long, and bend each one in half to form a hairpin shape. Tape two U-ends onto the base of each of the three candles.

4 Place the three candles in a triangular formation in the block of floral foam, anchoring them in place with the wires.

5 Cut all the foliage into sprigs of approximately 6–8 inches (15–20 cm). Arrange the rosehips around the candles, pushing the stems into the floral foam.

6 Add the sprigs of blackberries and guelder rose in the same way, spacing them evenly over the arrangement.

7 Finally, use the sprigs of fruiting ivy to fill in all the gaps between the other berries, making sure that all the floral foam is concealed and that the display has a good shape with an even balance of color.

PROJECT 4

autumn wreath

Rich red and orange beech leaves have been used to construct this beautifully glowing autumn wreath that would look fantastic either hung on a front door or else simply propped up on a shelf or mantelpiece. Use glycerined leaves, available from specialist florists, as this method of drying plant materials captures seasonal colors and prevents dried leaves from becoming dull and brittle, so that they will look stunning for six months or more.

MATERIALS & EQUIPMENT

for a wreath 20 inches (50 cm) in diameter:

30 lengths honeysuckle vine (*Lonicera*),
5 feet (1.6 m)

20 branches glycerined beech leaves (*Fagus*)

florist's scissors • reel wire • wire cutters

medium-gauge stub wires

heavy-gauge stub wire

1 To make a circular frame, bend 30 lengths of flexible honeysuckle vine into a circle. As you work, bind the stems together with a continuous length of spool wire. Pull the wire taut to make the binding tight and secure.

2 Cut sprigs of beech leaves from the large branches, so their woody stems are about 1 inch (2.5 cm) long. Arrange the sprigs in groups of three and wire them on double-leg mounts. To do this, hold a medium-gauge stub wire behind the group of stems and bend it into a hairpin, making one leg longer than the other. Wrap the long leg of wire around the stems and other leg of wire at least three times, then bring the wires together. Wire up about 150 sprigs into 50 bunches.

3 Hold a wired-up bunch of leaves, glossy side down, at an angle to the frame. Push the stub wires through the vine frame. Bend the group of leaves back on itself so that they face glossy side up. Tuck the wire ends into the back of the frame. Repeat with the next group of leaves, placing them 1¼ inches (3 cm) from the first group so that they overlap.

4 Continue working in the same direction, adding groups of wired-up leaves every 1¼ inches (3 cm) and turning the wreath as you go. In addition to attaching bunches along the top edge, start adding groups of beech leaves to the left and right of center, to fill in the inner and outer edges of the frame.

5 As you work, introduce a mix of different-colored beech leaves here and there to make the display look as natural as possible.

6 When you have worked your way around the frame, check for gaps and fill them in where necessary. Gently lift the leaves away from the frame to make the display look fuller. To hang the finished wreath, insert a heavy-gauge stub wire through the wreath back and twist the ends together. Dust at regular intervals to keep the display looking its best.

Cozy enough for an intimate supper for two, but spacious enough for a family meal or Sunday lunch with friends, a cottage-style dining space can suit more or less any occasion. The first requirement is a large, unpretentious wooden table. Next, a selection of chairs, ladder- or spindle-backed, rush-seated or upholstered—and they don't necessarily have to match. Gentle but adequate lighting will set the scene: either a chandelier or an old-fashioned rise-and-fall lamp would be a good choice, or you could

dining rooms

opt for the flickering glow of candles. Underfoot, durable wipeable flooring is most practical, but it needn't be boring—oiled or painted floorboards are lovely. And on the walls, pale colors will make the room seem airy and light, while darker shades add atmosphere and drama.

TOP, LEFT *This circular table is simple and charming, while the central pendant adds a gentle glow at night.*

TOP, RIGHT *Rush-seated chairs and a handful of ceramic accessories bring a farmhouse atmosphere even to a room that is otherwise rather bare.*

BOTTOM, LEFT *Differing patterns of checks and stripes in a harmonizing color add a charming variety to this cottage-style dining room. It would be*

easy to make loose seat covers such as this, adding extra-long ties as a quirky decorative feature.

BOTTOM, CENTER *Cover a dining table with a large piece of fabric (a sheet will do) for instant prettiness.*

BOTTOM, RIGHT *Mismatching chairs aren't a problem with this style, though if you prefer a more cohesive look, you could always paint them all the same color.*

colors & textures

Comfort is a priority in a dining room, as this is a space where you'll want to linger over a delicious meal in an atmosphere that's conducive to relaxation and enjoyment. Of course, everyone's idea of comfort is different, so for some a dining room should be decorated in fresh, pale colors to create a cool and airy feel; for others, deeper, bolder shades strike the right note of warmth and intimacy. Either style can look gorgeous and will fit perfectly with a country-cottage look.

When planning your color scheme, remember that your dining table will be the focal point of the room. If you want to leave it uncovered, take your cue from the color of its surface—pale or dark wood, sanded, polished, or perhaps even painted, or covered with self-adhesive plastic. Paler woods such as beech and ash, or woods that have been limewashed or painted in a pale color, tend to lend themselves to light and airy color schemes, such as clean white, soft cream, dove gray, or a pale blue, pink, yellow, or lilac.

TOP, LEFT *The blue and white checkerboard floor is the most eye-catching element of this simple dining room. It is fairly easy to create the same effect, using either linoleum or vinyl tiles, or by carefully painting wooden boards with two colors of floor paint.*

TOP, CENTER *Deep colors can bring a great sense of comfort and intimacy to a dining room, and a bottle green such as this is highly effective, especially combined with the warm wood of the floor and furniture. The pale woodwork and checked fabrics offset the dramatic color so that it is not overly imposing.*

TOP, RIGHT *There is something very appealing about an all-white dining room, probably to do with its associations of lightness and cleanliness. White can look very stark and modern, but here the furniture is traditional, the seats are padded, and the twinkling chandelier above is delightfully traditional and pretty.*

RIGHT *There is a wonderful mix of textures in this room, from the stone floor to the linen blind, the wooden chairs to the white tablecloth. It is unforced and easy, a charming example of the cottage look at its best.*

LEFT *The deep reddish-brown on this wall has very earthy overtones and creates a strong impression—warm, dramatic, and rather appealing. This may be an informal spot in which to have the odd bite, but it is nevertheless very inviting.*

ABOVE AND RIGHT *Vivid red and yellow have been used in this room as an accent against an otherwise neutral scheme comprising natural wood and white-painted walls. They add a note of vibrant good cheer to what is otherwise quite a formal setting.*

Darker woods, on the other hand, work extremely well with dramatic colors such as ocher, bottle green, navy, or a classic "dining room" red. Choose dining chairs that work with your theme—or, if you have chairs that don't quite look right, make slipcovers for them using inexpensive fabric. Use paint or wallpaper to enhance the walls, and if your floor needs attention as well, you can transform it quickly and easily either by painting boards with floor paint or putting down a colorful rug.

Another way in which you can establish a welcoming atmosphere is by using contrasting textures, making sure that you include enough softness—cushions, tablecloths, rugs, lampshades, and window treatments—to counteract the hardness of tables, chairs, and storage. Other textures will mix in easily—the glitter of cut glass, the glaze of ceramics, the shine of flatware, and the delicacy of fresh flowers—and the result will be a room that both looks gorgeous and feels delightful.

FAR LEFT, TOP *Making a patchwork tablecloth is a wonderful way to use up remnants of fabric, and it adds a cheerful, colorful note to any dining area.*

FAR LEFT, CENTER *Checked fabrics in the same colorway always coordinate nicely, and look just right in a country-style dining room. This sweet little fruit container has been made by simply covering some cardboard with left-over fabric and adding ties at the corners.*

FAR LEFT, BOTTOM *Plump cushions add greatly to the comfort of this bench seat, and the understated fabric is a lovely choice for the covers.*

LEFT, ABOVE *Panels of sheer fabric, with softly gathered valances above, diffuse the light and bring an ethereal quality to this dining room.*

LEFT, BELOW *Layering cloth upon cloth, mixing plains, patterns, and different colors is an effective way of introducing an interesting table dressing.*

RIGHT *A close-up of this patchwork cloth shows the intricacy of its pattern—a real heirloom.*

fabrics

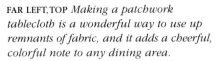

It is hard to overestimate the importance of fabric in a dining room, where fluid, draping textures are vital in creating an intimate and relaxing atmosphere and to counterpoint the hard surfaces of tables, chairs, china, and flatware. Fabric in appealing colors and patterns will bring interest and comfort, while touches such as ribbon ties or appliqué add a delightfully thoughtful and personal element.

Your tablecloth will often be a focal point, and the fabric and style you choose for it will help set the tone for the whole room. A bright floral, large or small checks, or a patchwork of coordinating patterns would all be pretty; solid colors could be given a country-style twist with the addition of a ruched edging, a trim made from rickrack or ribbon, or some appliquéd motifs. If you prefer not to use a tablecloth, you can create an interesting display with a long, narrow runner laid along the center of the table. Place mats and napkins will add to the pretty effect—they could be made from remnants of patterned fabric, or in a plain fabric embellished

with beads, buttons, ribbons, embroidery, or appliqué. Pick a consistent color theme, but mix and match pattern with pattern, and pattern with plain for an individual overall look.

Another key choice is fabric for the window dressings: perhaps a panel of pale, floaty voile with a gathered valance, a jolly cotton check curtain with tied tops, or a heavy expanse of dark velvet. Alternatively, a roman shade made from an informal fabric such as linen or denim can look beautiful. Again, trims, gathered edgings, ruffles, patchwork, and appliqué will all add to the effect.

Most dining chairs will benefit from the addition of a soft cushion pad. Don't try too hard to match this fabric exactly with that of the tablecloth—an eclectic combination is far more appropriate to cottage style, provided the colors complement each other and the patterns don't clash. This is your opportunity to use up

fabric remnants in imaginative ways—even old tea towels (as long as they're not threadbare) could be given a new lease on life, while very small pieces could be made up as a length of patchwork and then sewn together. Chairs that don't quite work in the scheme, or that are badly in need of freshening up, can be transformed with a slipcover, in either plain cotton or muslin, or made from a patterned calico fabric that adds a spot of lively color without great expense.

CLOCKWISE, FROM LEFT *A simple blind in a neutral color can be given extra interest with a decorative border, an unusual pull, or—as here—a tie-top.*

Bright seat pads introduce comfort and color into an otherwise rather austere, all-white room.

Layering one fabric on top of another can have interesting results. Here, a long, thin runner with a pretty pattern has been placed on top of a plain tablecloth.

For the epitome of simplicity, use a white or cream tablecloth with curtains in the same fabric—you can prevent them from looking too plain by making sure that they are generously gathered.

For a really pretty country effect, line a cupboard door with gathered panels of gingham.

A pleasant mix of informal fabrics in typically country-style colors and patterns makes this dining area laidback and inviting.

PROJECT 5

floral tablecloth

Making this tablecloth is a practical and delightful way to use up remnants of chintz, gingham, and other printed upholstery fabrics. It is made from four striped triangles that create a pattern of concentric squares. Although the selection of fabrics in this example might appear random, it is carefully limited to three main colors—pink, blue, and cream—which gives cohesion and unity to the overall design.

MATERIALS & EQUIPMENT

selection of upholstery fabric

white thread

squared pattern paper

pencil • yardstick

fabric scissors

tailor's chalk

needle

sewing machine

MAKING THE TEMPLATE

1 Mark a triangle on the pattern paper. Draw a baseline 60 inches (150 cm) long, mark the midpoint and draw a 30 inch (75 cm) line at right angles. Add two lines joining the ends of the baseline to the top of the shorter line (see below), then cut out the template.

MAKING THE TRIANGLES

2 Cut four strips of fabric measuring 4 x 60 inches (10 x 150 cm) each. These will form the border of the tablecloth. Fold each strip in half widthwise and mark the center with tailor's chalk. Cut four strips measuring 4 x 52 inches (10 x 134 cm) from contrasting fabric to make the next round. Mark the midpoints.

3 With right sides together, pin and baste one long and one shorter strip together, matching the chalk marks (see step 2). Machine-stitch ½ inch (1 cm) from the edge, then neaten the raw edges with an overlock stitch or zigzag. Press the seam allowance toward the longer strip. Join the other strips in pairs in the same way.

4 The next four strips are 4 x 46 inches (10 x 118 cm). Cut out, mark the centers, and sew to the previous strips as before. Continue adding strips of fabric (see steps 2 and 3), reducing the length each time by 6 inches (16 cm), until each triangle is complete, with ten stripes. You can vary the width of the strips slightly to give variety.

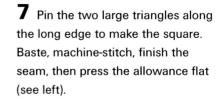

JOINING THE TRIANGLES

5 Pin the paper template to a finished triangle, lining up the long edges, and cut out the fabric (see step 2). Cut out the other three pieces in the same way.

6 With right sides together, pin two triangles along one short edge, carefully matching the seams. Baste and machine-stitch, leaving a ½ inch (1 cm) seam allowance. Finish the raw edges and press the seam to one side. Join the other two triangles in the same way.

7 Pin the two large triangles along the long edge to make the square. Baste, machine-stitch, finish the seam, then press the allowance flat (see left).

FINISHING

8 To finish the edge, press under a ½ inch (1 cm) hem around the border, then press the border in half so that the folded edge lines up with the first seam.

9 Finish each corner with a miter. Unfold the deeper turning and fold the corner over at an angle of 45° so that the creases line up to form a right angle.

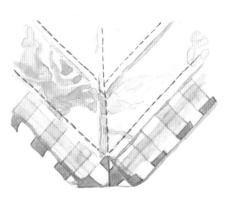

10 Refold the turnings, press lightly, and pin the fold to the wrong side, so that it conceals the first seam allowance. Baste in place, then slipstitch the two sides of each miter together, starting at the point and working inward. Hand stitch the hem to the cloth, sewing through the seam allowance so the stitches do not show through on the right side. Press the hem.

Dining tables, sideboards, hutch, or cabinets are all the most fantastic surfaces on which to make a stunning display of pretty and practical accessories. It could be utterly simple—a pot of fresh flowers or a bowl of pine cones placed in the center of the table, for example—or slightly more formal, such as a neat row of herbs or spring bulbs in a variety of planters. Or it could be lavish—a profusion of flowers, fruit, vegetables, or preserves, shown off in the prettiest of ceramic, enamel, glass, wood, or wirework containers.

When setting the table, there are lots of lovely ways to create an informal, attractive scene. Perhaps a small sprig of herbs or leaves, held together with a twist of string and placed on a dinner plate, or a placecard of handmade paper with elegant calligraphy. Or, for a sweetly pretty effect, you could attach a silk flower to a napkin ring with wire, or even sprinkle dried rose petals over the entire table.

finishing touches

OPPOSITE, ABOVE LEFT *Fruit and vegetables make a glorious display in their own right—there's no need to think too carefully about how to set them out.*

OPPOSITE, ABOVE RIGHT *Spring bulbs in assorted pretty planters are a gorgeous centerpiece in this informal country kitchen.*

OPPOSITE, BELOW LEFT *Placing a sprig of lavender on a folded napkin is an appealing finishing touch for a table setting.*

OPPOSITE, BELOW RIGHT *All sorts of containers can be used for attractive displays in the dining room, from ceramic or glass to wood or wirework.*

ABOVE *One of the key ideas in cottage style is to create a feeling of abundance, and this bowl, which is burgeoning with foliage, is just right.*

LEFT *These patchwork place mats are simply delightful, and the beaded milk-jug cover is a lovely old-fashioned touch.*

PROJECT 6

hop centerpiece

Hops are evocative of the countryside at harvest time, so they are the obvious choice for any arrangement made to celebrate this time of year. This attractive rustic display is surprisingly simple to make—all you need for the basic structure are a sturdy metal ring and four large pillar candles. Natural sisal rope is used to tie the ring to the outside of the candles that support it, providing a frame onto which the textural fresh hops can be bound with wire.

MATERIALS & EQUIPMENT

4 candles, 8 x 4 inches
(20 x 10 cm) diameter

1 metal ring wreath frame, 15 inches
(38 cm) diameter

6 yards (6 m) sisal rope, ¼ inch
(5 mm) diameter

1 vine hops (*Humulus lupulus*),
for approximately 70 sprigs,
8 inches (20 cm) long

florist's scissors • fine-gauge gold wire

wire cutters

1 Once complete, this candle arrangement will be difficult to move around, so either assemble it in situ or on a small tray or wooden board. Lay the metal ring flat on your surface and stand the four candles inside it, evenly spaced apart.

2 Cut the sisal rope into four lengths of 60 inches (150 cm). Wind one piece four times around one of the candles, roughly 3 inches (8 cm) from the base. Put one end of the rope through the metal ring and tie a secure double knot.

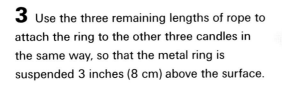

3 Use the three remaining lengths of rope to attach the ring to the other three candles in the same way, so that the metal ring is suspended 3 inches (8 cm) above the surface.

4 Cut the hops into approximately 70 sprigs, 8 inches (20 cm) long. Lay the first sprig along the ring and bind the stalk to it with gold wire.

5 Gradually build up the decoration by adding more sprigs of hops to the ring, overlapping them and binding them in place with gold wire as before, until the metal ring is completely hidden.

6 Finally, cut some short stems of hops and push the stalks directly into the arrangement. Make sure to fill any gaps and conceal any visible wire.

The kitchen is the focal point of every cottage-style home, providing not just a practical place for cooking, but also a welcoming space for family to gather, for children to play or do homework, for doing laundry, watching television, or just chatting to friends. Get the basics right—good appliances sited in convenient positions, tough flooring, and plenty of work space—and you can have fun with the rest.

kitchens

Storage, for example, need not be rows of boring built-ins, but could consist of a large pine hutch, supplemented by open shelves, hanging racks, assorted cupboards and chests, and wicker baskets. Install concealed lighting to work by and add atmospheric wall lights and chandeliers for decorative effect, and finish off with pretty paint colors and country-style accessories.

CLOCKWISE, FROM TOP LEFT
Open storage can be a really effective way to introduce a country look to your kitchen; just make sure you're prepared to keep it relatively neat, or else add a few cupboards in which to hide your messy stuff. A rise-and-fall pendant is useful over a large work surface and has a homey, traditional look. Wicker baskets of all shapes and sizes provide handy storage and bring a rustic look to the kitchen. A cheap alternative to built-in cupboard fronts—a simple panel of fabric (in whatever color or pattern suits your room) threaded over a wire or slender pole. Warm terracotta flagstones set the scene in this appealing room, while a combination of built-in cabinets and open shelving is both practical and attractive.

ABOVE *It's easy to give painted furniture an aged, distressed appearance. Simply rub the corners and edges unevenly with a wax candle, then cover with a coat of paint—the waxed areas will retain their original surface and the over-all effect will be nicely worn.*

RIGHT *Using a strong color gives a kitchen a very definite personality—and in this room not only the walls are painted red, but also the tongue and groove ceiling and the woodwork around the windows.*

colors & textures

A cottage-style kitchen is the heart of the home, the center of family life, and in this room a sense of warmth, comfort, intimacy and easy relaxation is essential. Color can be quite strong—anything from buttercup yellow to tomato red. Blues or greens can also look gorgeous, while cream is a traditional choice for those who prefer more subtle shades. White combined with another color, such as lemon yellow or cornflower blue, is another pretty option, and don't forget that you can keep background colors plain and still add a great deal of vitality in the form of accessories such as gleaming copper pots and pans, blue and white china, or brightly colored glassware.

ABOVE *You can pick up informal, country-style kitchenware really cheaply in thrift stores, garage sales, and auctions. Choose pieces that are complementary in shape and shade, and create a pretty display on a shelf or flat surface. If you come across a beat up old cupboard, too, it is often possible to transform it by painting it, changing the knobs or handles, and perhaps even replacing the door panels with chicken wire or fabric.*

LEFT *Whether it's mugs, bread crocks, saucepans, or soup spoons, you can make a display of practically any kitchen equipment. A neat row of identical—or near identical—objects on a shelf or tabletop always looks good.*

LEFT *A stone floor is a beautiful base for a country kitchen, utterly traditional and full of character. This one is made of randomly sized flag stones, which adds to its impact.*

ABOVE, LEFT *White and soft blue makes an appealing combination, with no need for any further embellishment.*

ABOVE *Another version of a blue and white kitchen, with plain wooden furniture and simple checked fabric used in gathered panels to line the cupboard doors.*

OPPOSITE, ABOVE *The intricate patterns and vibrant color of these striking tiles is all that is needed to make a dramatic impact in this otherwise very simple kitchen. By scouring thrift stores and reclamation yards, you may be able to put together a collection of mismatching (but nevertheless coordinating) tiles that could be used in a similar way.*

OPPOSITE, BELOW *Create an eclectic and appealing combination of textures by using natural materials such as wood, wicker, stone, slate, glass, ceramics, and metal. Wicker baskets such as these are a nicely informal way to contain assorted items neatly on shelves without enclosing them behind closed doors.*

To start with, a quick coat of latex on the walls will go
a long way toward establishing the right atmosphere.
Choose paint with a high proportion of pigment for an
intense effect, or else a chalky surface texture for a softer,
more historic look. The color and texture of your cupboard
doors will make as big an impact as those of the walls, and
it is important to get them right. Modern units with their
man-made, smooth, glossy finishes are simply inappropriate,
but there are many ways to disguise them. Use cupboard
paint as a primer and then add color in the form of an
eggshell top coat. To break up its solid effect you could
use a paint technique such as colorwashing, distressing,
ragging, dragging, or sponging—they would all create
a charming, authentic look and introduce a nicely worn
surface texture. Apply the same techniques to give new
life to old wooden furniture, too, from hutches and tables
to chairs and cupboards. To complete the effect, appliances,
radiators, and even tiled backsplashes can be transformed
with a careful application of specialized paint.

PROJECT 7

plate rack

If you are a little bit handy with a saw and hammer, you'll enjoy making this Swedish-style plate rack. It would traditionally have been used to display the family's finest dishes, but will look equally pretty stacked with a few charmingly mismatched plain and printed plates. You can finish it in any way you like to complement your kitchen.

MATERIALS & EQUIPMENT

enough 7½ x 60 inch (19 x 150 cm) reclaimed wood, such as floorboarding or softwood, to cut the following pieces:

2 33 inch (85.5 cm) lengths, for sides; 1 24 inch (60 cm) length, for bottom shelf

7½ x 20 inches (19 x 50 cm) reclaimed wood or softwood, cut as follows:

3 24 inch (60 cm) lengths, for shelves

½ x 1 inch (12.5 x 25 mm) softwood, cut as follows:

4 24 inch (60 cm) lengths, for rails

1 24 inch (60 cm) length, for bottom rail

tracing paper • pencil • C-clamps

coping saw or jigsaw

medium and fine sandpaper

wood glue • brads • hammer

try square or carpenter's level

4 wall attachments (with screws)

screwdriver

wire wool

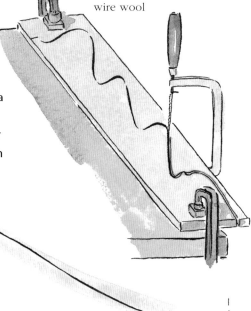

1 On a photocopier, enlarge the template (below) for the two sides by 200 percent. Transfer the shape onto each of the two rectangular side pieces, making sure you mark the shelf positions on the inside faces.

2 With C-clamps, clamp each piece of wood in turn to the edge of a workbench or a sturdy table and cut out the shapes using a coping saw or jigsaw. Sand the sawn curves smooth to remove any jagged edges.

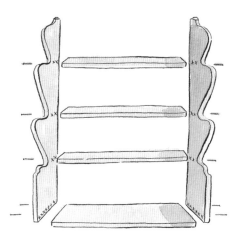

3 The shelves sit between the shaped sides, flush with the straight back edge. Attach them using wood glue and brads, inserted from the outside of the side sections. Start with the wider bottom shelf, positioning it level with the bottom edges of the sides. Next, attach the three remaining shelves, lining them up with the marks made in step 1. Use a try square or carpenter's level to check that they are level and square to the sides.

4 Glue and pin the rails in position. This is done working from the front. Start with the bottom rail, fitting it in between the two sides and flush with the front edge of the bottom shelf to form a step. The other four rails are fitted on the outside edges of the curved sides. Position three of them across each of the widest sections of the top three curves and sit the final one at the very top of the rack, tucking it behind the highest curve.

5 The position of both shelves and rails can be adjusted to fit any size of plate so that you can have smaller plates on the higher shelves, for example. Simply raise or lower them to a suitable height to house your display.

6 To finish the wood, paint or wax to suit your decor. Rub the rack all over with sandpaper and steel wool to achieve a smooth surface.

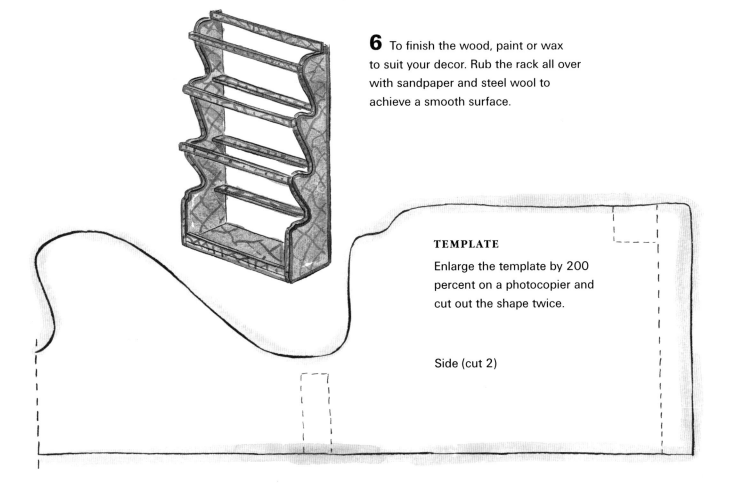

TEMPLATE

Enlarge the template by 200 percent on a photocopier and cut out the shape twice.

Side (cut 2)

fabrics

Fabrics play an important role in a country-style kitchen, introducing an essential element of softness, texture, color, and pattern. These are unfussy fabrics, however—whatever you choose may be as pretty as a picture, but should also be workmanlike, durable, and unpretentious. Cotton, linen, canvas, ticking, and denim are all good choices, while voile can work well for screening windows and wipeable oilcloth is ideal for covering tables—especially ones that regularly play host to children's painting or sticking sessions. As a starting point, choose colors that complement your overall scheme—you can't go wrong with sunny yellow, bright red, mid blue, soft green, white, or cream—and patterns that have stood the test of time, such as checks, ginghams, spriggy florals, or simple stripes.

When designing window treatments, you must avoid hanging flapping curtains anywhere near cooking areas, and these are best kept away from sinks, too. Instead, opt for a neat little blind that won't dangle in the way. If you make it in a cheerful floral, it

ABOVE *These pretty curtains are gathered over a slim pole. Their jolly colors are a lively embellishment to the room.*

BELOW, LEFT *Here, a cupboard with plain glass doors has been given a pretty decorative treatment with the addition of panels of broad-striped fabric attached to the inside.*

BELOW, RIGHT *Don't forget that even the humblest of towels can make an attractive addition to your scheme, while an old chair can be disguised with a throw made from a comfortable old blanket.*

OPPOSITE, CLOCKWISE FROM BOTTOM RIGHT *Simple fabric has been used for a pretty tablecloth in a kitchen-diner. Make a café curtain from a small remnant of fabric— even a dish towel. Add tab tops or ties, and thread over a metal or bamboo pole. These diaphanous curtains are ultra-plain, except for the pretty gathered valance with a sassy red trim. Casual fabrics look great in a kitchen, and for this simple curtain two remnants have been stitched together and jazzed up with the addition of some appliquéd flowers. Tiny patches of assorted fabrics have been used to create this fabulously eccentric tea cozy.*

BELOW, LEFT *This ruched red blind is a good idea behind a sink—decorative but not so flouncy that it will get wet.*

BELOW, RIGHT *A simple, pointed edging adds a lovely, country-style feel to a plain shelf. The matching tea towels below are another nice touch.*

OPPOSITE, ABOVE *An utterly simple solution to the problem of hiding things you don't want seen, without spending*

too much money—a gathered panel of plain fabric hung in front of open shelves.

OPPOSITE, BELOW, FROM LEFT TO RIGHT *Fabric-covered notebooks can be made by hand by covering ready-made books with remnants of linen or cotton, adding a monogrammed patch and some pretty ties. They can be used for recipes, dinner-party notes, or just*

plain shopping lists. Use tiny scraps of fabric to cover the lids of jam jars— gingham is traditional, but plains can look equally attractive. There's no reason why oven mitts should be plain and boring. If you can't find a pretty pair in the shops, you could make some yourself, using tough, thick fabric and plenty of wadding inside as heat-proofing.

will still be perky and pretty. Alternatively, add some interest with a patterned border, a scalloped bottom edge, or a ruched pelmet above. At windows or doors that are free from obstruction, you can go to town with generous lengths of fabric that will add immense country-cottage charm.

Gathered panels of fabric also make a pleasantly informal alternative to the conventional cupboard door. Simply hang from an elasticized wire or a slender pole in front of open shelves to screen whatever is on them. You can use fabric to line cupboard doors and to edge the fronts of shelves, too. For a fun,

personal touch make accessories such as egg cozies, tea cozies, or jam jar covers from whatever bits of fabric you can lay your hands on; you may also want to hang a cross-stitch sampler on a wall as a pretty adornment.

And, finally, there are the fabrics without which a kitchen simply would not function—dish towels and oven gloves. These are essentially utilitarian, and as such must be practical and fit for their jobs, but that's no reason why they can't also be attractive in themselves, in patterns and colors that complement and enhance the overall look and feel of the room.

MATERIALS & EQUIPMENT

3 different main fabrics

lining fabric

⅝ inch (1.5 cm) wide red braid

PROJECT 8

yellow-checked curtains

These cheerful curtains are guaranteed to bring a relaxed, sunny atmosphere to any room. They use panels of three co-ordinating fabrics joined horizontally, with vivid scarlet braid sewn over the seams to conceal them. The bold checks and trim have a pleasing, rustic simplicity that is echoed by the simple ties that hold the curtains to an iron pole.

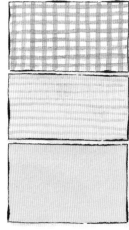

1 Measure the window to calculate fabric quantities (see page 104). Each panel occupies one third of the drop of the finished curtain. Add ⅝ inch (1.5 cm) to each panel for each seam. Add 3 inches (8 cm) to the top panel for the heading and 6½ inches (16 cm) to the bottom panel for the hem. Each curtain must be the width of the pole plus 5 inches (12 cm) for side hems. The lining must be 1¾ inches (4 cm) smaller than the finished curtain all around. Cut out the fabric.

2 Place the top panel on a flat surface with the middle panel on top, right sides together and raw edges aligned. Pin, baste, and machine stitch the two panels together, using a ⅝ inch (1.5 cm) seam allowance and matching the checks as best you can. Press open the seam. Attach the bottom panel to the middle panel in the same way.

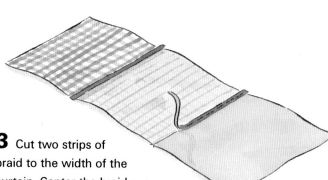

3 Cut two strips of braid to the width of the curtain. Center the braid over the seams between the panels on the right side of the curtain. Pin, baste and machine-stitch down both edges of the braid.

4 Press a 2½ inch (6 cm) hem at each side of the curtain and a double 3 inch (8 cm) hem at the bottom. Press in the angled miters (see page 105). Pin and baste the hems in place. Herringbone-stitch the side hems. Slipstitch the base hem and the miters.

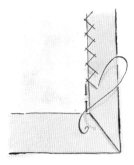

5 Cut out the lining. Press a ¾ inch (2 cm) hem along each side edge and a ¾ inch (2 cm) double base hem. Pin and baste the hems. Miter the corners (see page 105) and machine-stitch the hems in place.

6 Place the curtain on a flat surface, wrong side up. Place the lining on top, right side up. Match the corners of the lining with the mitered corners of the curtain and align the top raw edges. Pin the curtain and lining together along the top raw edges. Pin and baste the lining to the curtain. Slipstitch the lining to the curtain fabric. Leave the bottom of the lining open—the curtain will hang better.

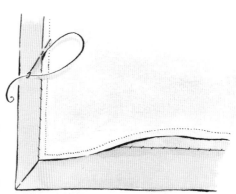

7 The number of ties needed will depend on the width of the curtain. There should be one tie every 10 inches (25 cm). Cut a strip of fabric 2½ x 20 inches (6 x 50 cm) for each tie. Make up the ties (see page 105), knotting the ends of each one.

8 Lay the curtain flat, right side up. Using fabric pen, lightly mark a line 3 inches (8 cm) below the top raw edge. Place a tie at each top corner of the curtain and space the other ties at 10 inch (25 cm) intervals between. Pin and baste the halfway point of each tie to the marked line, then machine-stitch all the way along the line, taking in the ties as you go.

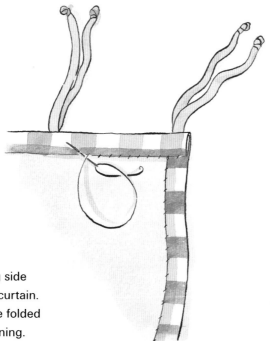

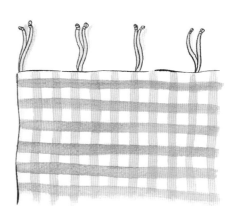

9 Press in a double 4 cm (1¾ inch) fold to the wrong side along the top edges of the curtain. Pin, baste, and slipstitch the folded edge of the curtain to the lining.

10 Working at the two top corners of the curtain, slipstitch the open ends of the top hem together. Press the finished curtains, then tie them to the pole with loose bows.

LEFT *Large wicker baskets make useful storage and can be tucked away neatly under a table, as here. They are also delightfully traditional and add country charm to any kitchen.*

BELOW, LEFT *Painted mugs can be used as decorative accessories as well as for cups of coffee.*

BELOW, RIGHT *Even plain kitchen utensils can be turned into a beautiful display—these wooden spoons and spatulas are easily accessible for a busy cook, but look great popped into a row of matched white pots.*

OPPOSITE, ABOVE LEFT *This pretty pitcher has been put to good use as a holder for kitchen implements. The tiles in the background are casually mismatching but terribly pretty.*

OPPOSITE, ABOVE RIGHT *Use a mantelpiece, windowsill, or other flat surface to display stoneware, glassware, or other attractive kitchen necessities.*

OPPOSITE, BELOW *Country style is unforced and understated, but with the right mix of useful and attractive objects—just easy-going, simple, and traditional—you will naturally arrive at the right look.*

finishing touches

Whatever colors, textures, and fabrics you have used to create the backbone of your kitchen scheme, it is the finishing touches that will pull everything together and give the room real heart and soul. Not all finishing touches are last-minute accessories, however—here you will find that practical, everyday items can not only be useful for cooking, but also for creating charming and informal displays that really add to the overall atmosphere.

If you have wall-to-wall, floor-to-ceiling built-in cupboards, it is worth considering removing one or two and replacing them with some open shelves. You may even be lucky enough to have a traditional hutch, a butcher's block, a mantel-piece, or a spacious windowsill—you simply need a surface on which you can casually arrange potted herbs, antique glasses, stoneware jugs, chintz-printed china, or the like. From hooks, peg rails, or metal bars you can hang pans, implements, dish towels, chopping boards, and so on, while on the floor you can stack baskets and boxes.

Although the essence of country style is an unplanned, unforced look, it is still worth considering how you can arrange things so that they are shown to their best advantage. Shiny modern appliances are, ideally, kept behind closed doors, as are unexciting cans of food, plastic lidded boxes, and anything else that either offers little visual interest or is just plain unattractive. Then group together items that are good-looking singly or en masse—a wooden spoon, for example, might be boring on its own, but could look great popped into a jug with several others and stood beside the cooktop or on a nearby shelf. Rows of white plates could be stacked on shelves, interspersed with colored crockery or vases of flowers, while colored dish towels could be hung from a Shaker-style peg rail. Even utilitarian objects such as cheese graters, bread boards, colanders, or soup ladles, as long as they're not too sleek and modern in style, can become delightful decorative accessories when displayed in a way that is usable but that also emphasizes their inherent charm.

ABOVE, LEFT AND RIGHT *The owner of this house has created a work surface in a hutch from what is in fact simply a small table with some shelving above. She has used an all-white scheme, which contrasts beautifully with the warm old wood, while the natural colors of foliage, fruit, and vegetables add a dash of vibrancy.*

OPPOSITE, ABOVE *A Shaker-style peg rail is a practical way to store often-used items close at hand, while at the same time showing off their interesting shapes, colors, and textures.*

OPPOSITE, BELOW, FROM LEFT TO RIGHT *Simplicity itself: a chopping board with a heart shape cut-out so that it can be hung easily. These wire implements are unlikely to be used very often, but their graphic shapes make a fantastic display against the weathered wooden wall. On a sunny windowledge you can't beat a sweet display of herbs in mismatched but pretty pots.*

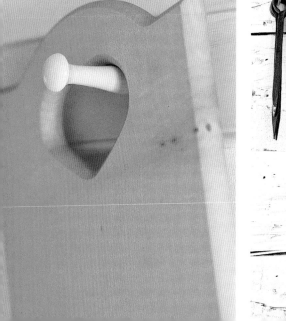

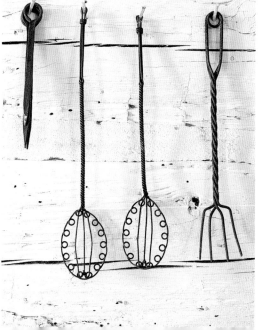

PROJECT 9

key cabinet

Finding keys can become a permanent pastime, unless you always return them to the same place. Keep them all in this shallow cabinet, which could hang on the wall, and you will never need to search for them again. If you have the wood cut to size by your supplier, the rest of the project is straightforward. The key design on the door can be painted freehand or with a stencil, using watered-down emulsion.

MATERIALS & EQUIPMENT

½ inch (12.5 mm) softwood,
cut as follows:
2 2 x 9½ inches (55 x 240 mm), for sides
2 2¾ x 8 inches (70 x 200 mm), for
base and top

¼ inch (6 mm) softwood, cut as follows:
2 1 x 9½ inches (25 x 240 mm), for
door frame sides
2 1 x 4½ inches (25 x 110 mm), for
door frame top and bottom

¼ inch (6 mm) plywood, cut as follows:
1 7¼ x 9½ inches (185 x 240 mm),
for back
1 6¼ x 9½ inches (160 x 240 mm),
for door panel

small strip of wood, 1¾ inches (43 mm)
length, for door stop

small door knob (with screw)

wood glue • brads • hammer

medium and fine sandpaper • awl

screwdriver • 2 butt hinges
(with screws)

8 cup hooks (with screws) for keys

hand drill with ⅙ inch (4 mm) screw bit

1 Butt the edges of the side panels up to the back piece and glue as shown. Reinforce with brads knocked in from the back.

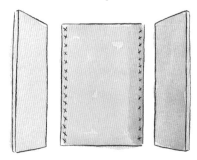

2 Apply glue to the underside of the assembled back and sides and attach them to the base. Position the base so that one long edge is flush with the back of the side panels, leaving an equal ⅓ inch (9 mm) overhang at both sides.

3 Apply glue to the top of the assembled cabinet and position the top section so that it corresponds exactly with the base—flush with the back and with a ⅓ inch (9 mm) overlap around the front and sides. Smooth all edges with medium, then fine sandpaper.

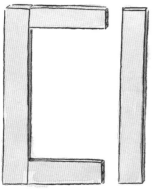

4 To make the door, assemble the frame pieces as shown, apply glue, and butt the pieces together.

5 Apply glue to the plywood door, as shown, then lay the assembled frame on top. Press together until the glue has bonded. Smooth the joined edges with sandpaper.

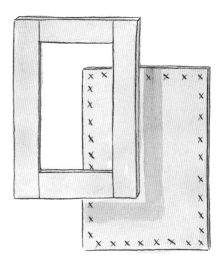

6 Next, attach the door knob; the one used here has a diameter of $7/8$ inch (22 mm). Make a pilot hole for the knob, using an awl, and screw it in place halfway down the right edge of the frame.

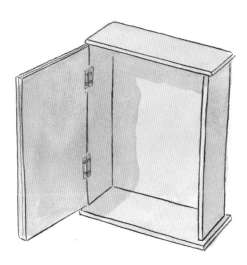

7 Position the hinges on the inside of the door as shown. Make pilot holes for the screws with an awl and screw in position. Check that the door closes properly without rubbing. Adjust the tightness of the screws if necessary, to make sure the door hangs evenly.

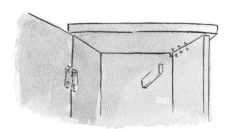

8 Glue a small piece of wood to the top inside of the right-hand panel, $1/2$ inch (12 mm) in from the front, so that the door will close in the correct position.

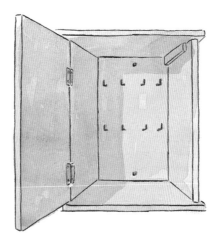

9 Using an awl, make pilot holes for the hooks. Position the hooks in two neat rows of four, with a gap in between to allow the keys to hang down. Screw the hooks in place. Mark two more holes through the entire thickness of the wood at the top and bottom of the rear panel for securing the cabinet to a wall. Use a hand drill fitted with a $1/6$ inch (4 mm) screw bit to drill the holes.

In a cottage-style bedroom, the emphasis is on creating a calm and pretty space which is as cozy for reading a book or watching television as it is conducive to a good night's sleep. Of course, a comfortable bed is the number-one priority, whether it is a four-poster, a curly-metal affair, a sleigh bed, or a plain divan. On the floor, many people like the feel of a soft carpet, although wooden floorboards with a few

bedrooms

rugs scattered about look lovely, too. Walls might be painted in soft, gentle colors to create a restful atmosphere, though darker shades, if you prefer them, can be warm and intimate. Storage is vital to avoid clutter—a capacious closet and a simple chest of drawers should suffice, and fabric furnishings provide the vital finishing touches, from curtains and bed canopies to bedcovers, quilts, and pillows.

CLOCKWISE, FROM CENTER: *Lace, frills, ribbons, and embroidery are all ideal to use as accessories in a very feminine, country-style bedroom. Creamy walls are the ideal background for a mix of fabrics in a variety of patterns. The austerity of this monochrome room, with dark metal bedsteads and white linen, is offset by the vibrant flowers beside the bed. The bold design of a patchwork quilt (relatively straightforward to make yourself) can be the focal point in an otherwise plain room. Intricate wooden rafters in this attic bedroom create such an interesting pattern and, with the floorboards, homey texture, that the rest of the decoration has been kept utterly simple. This room is pared down to the minimum, but all the essentials are there, and its strong colors and patterns add richness and vivacity.*

colors & textures

A cottage-style bedroom is the ultimate in comfort, while also being full of charm and character. The laidback, low-key nature of this look means that a sense of relaxation and intimacy is easy to achieve, especially with the right choice of colors and a good mix of textures.

Soft creams and pastels are ideal for paintwork on the walls: use a chalky, flat latex for a lovely effect, and either leave woodwork bare (stripped pine, rich mahogany, or waxed oak all look great) or cover it with satin gloss in a coordinating color. If you prefer wallpaper, pretty floral patterns—on a relatively small scale and, again, in faded colors—are ideal. You could even combine one papered wall with paintwork elsewhere. For those who prefer their colors stronger and richer, choose deep reds, purples, or blues, but avoid anything too harsh and bright: there's

OPPOSITE, ABOVE *A blue and white color scheme is unfussy and timeless, with masses of country charm. The unsophisticated nature of the striped cotton bedlinen has utilitarian appeal.*

OPPOSITE, BELOW *This is a warm, mustardy yellow that is neither too insipid nor too strong. It works well with the plain wooden furniture.*

ABOVE *Create interest in a bedroom by combining plain paintwork with one feature wall, whether it's covered in wallpaper or stenciled with a simple, pretty pattern. In this room the plaster walls have a fabulously rough, intriguing texture, while the armchair is delightfully shabby.*

ABOVE, RIGHT *An old, inexpensive cupboard can be transformed with a coat of paint and turned into an attractive feature of a bedroom—like this sweet bedside cabinet. The bed ends were made from two pieces of medium-density fiberboard that were cut into shape and hammered onto a broken bed.*

RIGHT *The bright-yellow walls of this bedroom are combined with fabrics in white, blue, pink, and green, including several different floral patterns and a checked blanket. It all blends into a fresh, eclectic, happy whole.*

LEFT *The natural color and texture of untreated wood is predominant in this informal room. Thick, soft bedding makes a nice contrast and creates a homey, inviting feel.*

ABOVE, LEFT *It's easy to add spots of color to an otherwise plain bedroom, simply by introducing a vivacious curtain, lamp, bedcover, or even a vase of flowers.*

ABOVE, RIGHT *The serenity of this light-filled eyrie is undisturbed—nothing but wood, white paint, and white linens.*

OPPOSITE, TOP *There is a variety of textures in this bedroom—from the thick curtain to the rough mirror frame, the wicker chair to the padded quilt—which bring subtle, sensual appeal.*

OPPOSITE, CENTER *Strong colors in the bedroom aren't for everyone, but if used carefully they can be wonderfully warm, cheerful, and inviting.*

OPPOSITE, BOTTOM *Smooth, plain, white bedlinen contrasts superbly with rough log-paneled walls in this rustic-meets-luxury country retreat.*

a fine line between warmth and brashness. Elsewhere in the room, flooring (whether carpets or wooden boards plus rugs), furniture, and fabrics should work with your basic scheme, but don't worry too much about making everything match perfectly—a mixture of colors has just the right casual and eclectic feel. Alternatively, go for simplicity by teaming white or off-white with just one other color—perhaps bright blue, lemon yellow, or rosy pink.

Finally, this is the place to experiment with secondhand finds that you can easily transform with a lick of paint or some fabric cheats. Throw an old blanket over a dilapidated chair or make a new pillow pad for a seat, repaint a bedstead, a lamp base, or a side table, and try your hand at stenciling a casual pattern across a chair back, on the lid of a blanket box, or over a cupboard door. It's surprisingly easy—the results don't have to be ultra-professional, just inventive, appealing, and attractive to live with.

MATERIALS & EQUIPMENT

rectangular wire frame,
18 x 24 inches (45 x 60 cm)

8 large pieces of driftwood

40 driftwood twigs

1 large, flat pebble

fine-grade sandpaper

spool wire • wire cutters

natural string • scissors

hot glue gun and glue sticks

picture hook (optional)

PROJECT 10

driftwood frame

Wood gnarled and bleached by the sun adds a primitive attraction to any interior, and half the fun of this creation is collecting the driftwood from a park or seashore. The beauty of this arrangement, which is put together on a rigid wire base, is that it is simple and inexpensive to produce, and works well as a unique and eye-catching detail against any backdrop, whether modern or traditional.

1 Lay out your pieces of driftwood and the rectangular wire frame on a flat, non-scratch surface. Decide the best way to arrange the wood on the frame; the largest piece will probably look best along the bottom edge. Using fine-grade sandpaper, smooth away any protrusions on the underside of the wood pieces so that they will lie flush with the frame.

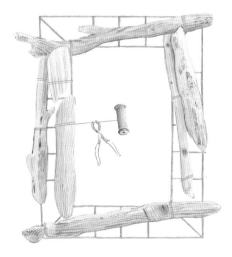

2 Using spool wire, bind each piece of wood securely onto the wire frame and then cut the wire with wire cutters. Fasten the longer pieces of wood at both ends, to hold them in position on the frame.

3 To disguise the sections where wood has been tied onto the frame with wire, wind natural string around the wire and fasten it in place with a double knot before cutting it with scissors.

4 Build up the driftwood frame by arranging smaller pieces of wood on top of the main structure. When you are happy that these smaller pieces fill in the gaps, glue them in place on the frame.

5 Finish the frame by gluing on small twigs. Use them to fill in any gaps between the larger pieces of wood and also to hide areas where the wire frame is still visible.

6 Finally, glue the large pebble onto the bottom left-hand corner of the frame. When the glue is dry, hang the frame on a nail, or tie a loop of wire to the frame and hang it from a strong picture hook.

fabrics

A combination of pretty fabrics makes the bedroom a sumptuously romantic, soft and feminine place to be. You can really go to town with sheets, bedspreads and covers, throws, cushions, pillows and bolsters, curtains, and accessories such as lavender sachets or pajama cases. When choosing fabrics, avoid patterns and colors that look too well matched in favor of a casual, eclectic mix. Combine inexpensive new fabrics with pieces picked up in secondhand stores or garage sales. And, if anything looks too bright and new, soak it in cold tea overnight for an instant aging effect.

The easiest way to start is with plain white sheets and pillowcases, adding a quilted or patchwork bedspread made from fabric remnants. This can be as simple as large squares or strips sewn together, or as complicated as the traditional pieced quilts that use a variety of cut-out shapes in complex patterns. Pile on throws (knitted, crocheted, lacy, or plain), blankets, and bedcovers, layering them in an easy,

OPPOSITE, TOP *Floral fabrics in soft colors are ideal for a bedroom. Here, a quilted bedcover is the focal point, while piles of pillows, in mismatched fabrics, have been added for a relaxed and cozy feel. The window treatment has been made from panels of plain white voile, hung loosely from a painted wooden pole.*

OPPOSITE, CENTER *Bolsters are easy to make and give a more structured look than squashy pillows.*

OPPOSITE, BOTTOM *A metal chair can be softened by the addition of a plump pillow.*

ABOVE *A lavender-sachet toy can be tied to a bed frame and makes a delightful accessory.*

LEFT, TOP *Lace, voile, frills, quilting, and delicate floral patterns are all ideal for the cottage-style bedroom. Plain walls and floors mean that the end result isn't over the top.*

LEFT, CENTER *Cover a small lidded box with a fabric remnant (glue it carefully, folding the edges in neatly) to make a jewelry box that's both pretty and useful.*

LEFT, BOTTOM *Use fabric generously for this look—here, a gathered dust ruffle fits around the base of the bed.*

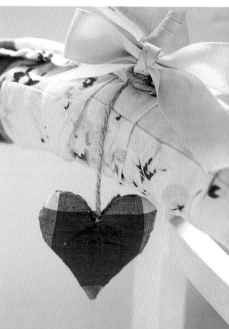

cozy way. Plenty of pillows and bolsters add atmosphere—make your own, using a mix of fabrics and trimming them with gathered edgings. Do the same for comfortable pillow pads and pretty slipcovers for bedside seating. Window treatments should be simple—either a roman or roll-up shade teamed with a fixed drape at either side of the window, or a pair of curtains, generously gathered and perhaps customized with a deep border of a different fabric, a contrast lining, or a trimming of ribbon or rickrack. Tabs or tie tops make an attractive, informal alternative to the usual curtain heading, though they can be slightly more awkward to draw.

If you need privacy during the day, pin up a panel of voile or gather a length of lace or sheer fabric over a slim wooden pole. Finish with accessories made from left-over scraps of fabric— anything from heart-shaped lavender sachets and knitted pajama cases to fabric-covered jewelry boxes and padded clothes hangers.

OPPOSITE, ABOVE *When mixing patterns, it's important to make sure that the colors you choose coordinate really well. The patchwork bedcover, gingham pillow and bolster, and checked curtains here are all in a cheerful middle red that is exactly right for this look.*

OPPOSITE, BELOW, FROM LEFT TO RIGHT *You can never have too many old-fashioned quilts, their faded colors and spriggy patterns a perfect embodiment of the best of country style. Florals and checks in the same color are both ideal fabrics for this look, and together they create a relaxed and appealing combination. Small scraps of fabric can be put to good use and turned into gorgeous accessories, such as this padded clothes hanger.*

ABOVE, LEFT *Layering fabrics is really effective—here, the owner has put dust ruffles with bedcovers, plus blankets, throws, and pillows.*

ABOVE, RIGHT *Toile de Jouy fabric, with its distinctive monochrome illustrations, is rather a grand fabric for this look, but this bedcover is softly comfortable and teamed with some mismatched pillows and a simple woven rug.*

PROJECT 11

patchwork duvet cover

The key to creating this beautiful duvet cover is to balance the colors—here, a lovely dusty pink combines perfectly with soft lilac, blue, and white. Although the sumptuous texture of the damask used here is gorgeous enough in itself, when choosing fabrics look out for details such as monograms, laundry marks, or makers' labels, which all make lovely features.

MATERIALS AND EQUIPMENT

selection of laundered damask napkins and tablecloths

white cotton double sheet

100 inches (2.5 m) woven tape

matching sewing thread

dressmaker's pins

sewing machine

sewing kit

CUTTING OUT

The instructions are for a double-bed sized duvet cover. Adjust the measurements accordingly to fit a larger or smaller duvet. Cut the back panel and facing from the sheet so that the existing hems lie along one short edge of the back panel and one long edge of the facing strip.

BACK PANEL

width = 80 inches (200 cm)

length = 92 inches (230 cm)

FACING

width = 2 inches (5 cm)

length = 80 inches (200 cm)

1 To make the front panel, trim off the hems and cut away any damaged areas from the napkins and tablecloths, to give a selection of strips and rectangles in different sizes. Lay the fabric out on the floor in an approximate 88 inch (220 cm) square, taking time to get a good balance of shape and color within the arrangement.

2 Start by sewing the smaller pieces together, then join them to form larger blocks, until the front is complete. Pin and baste each seam, then stitch ½ inch (1 cm) from the edge. Press the seam allowance to one side and topstitch ⅛ inch (3 mm) from the seam. Trim the finished panel to 80 inches (200 cm) square.

3 Pin and baste the facing strip along the bottom of the front panel so that the right side of the strip is against the wrong side of the panel. Stitch together along the bottom edge, ½ inch (1 cm) from the edge, then press the facing to the right side. Pin in place, then stitch along the same edge, ¼ inch (5 mm) from the seam, then top-stitch the edge of the facing to the cover.

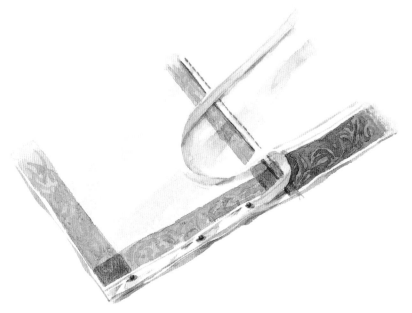

4 Press 12 inches (30 cm) along the hemmed edge of the back panel to the wrong side, making a deep turning.

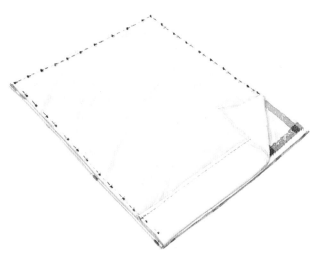

5 With the turning on the outside and right sides facing, pin and baste together the top and sides of the front and back panel together. Machine-stitch ¼ inch (5 mm) from the edge, then trim and neaten the seam allowance with a zigzag or overlocking stitch. Turn right side out and press.

6 Pin and baste the front and back panels together for 10 inches (25 cm) on each side of the opening and machine-stitch close to the edges.

7 Mark the positions of the ties by placing five pins at regular intervals along both edges of the opening.

8 Cut the tape into ten 10 inch (25 cm) lengths. Finish one end of each tie, then press under a narrow turning at the other end. Baste, then hand-stitch each tie securely in place on the inside of the cover.

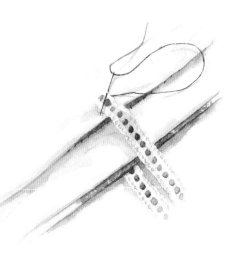

finishing touches

Once you've got the basics of the bedroom right, you can enjoy assembling the final elements that bring the room to life. You may wish to add all sorts of personal, individual touches, or simply leave the room quite plain, perhaps with just a glass jar full of flowers picked from the garden for a splash of color.

For practicality as well as prettiness, choose a mirror with an interesting frame—perhaps gilded, stenciled, or made from driftwood—and place it above the dressing table. A lamp beside the bed is essential, but make sure it has character and charm—if necessary, customize it by painting the base or attaching ribbon or beads to the shade. Even such simple things as laundry bags can be turned into an attractive display if made from lovely fabric and hung from a row of peg hooks. And for an appropriately natural, understated look, arrange leaves, feathers, shells, or pebbles on tabletops or shelves, where their colors and textures will add subtle decorative effect.

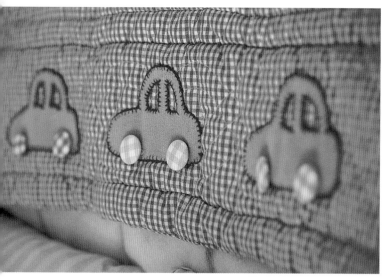

PROJECT 12

child's quilt

Crib quilts are popular gifts for new babies, who can lie on them when very small or be wrapped in them for outings. As the child grows, the quilt takes on a new role as a bedcover or play mat. This charming gingham quilt, with sweet appliquéd car motifs, continues a long-established custom and would undoubtedly make a very well-received present—if you can bear to give it away.

MATERIALS & EQUIPMENT

1 48 x 54 inch (120 x 135 cm) rectangle of polyester batting

2 43 x 50 inch (110 x 125 cm) rectangles of red gingham

drawing compass

thick tracing paper

sharp pencil

blue chalk dressmaker's pencil

yardstick

quilting thread or walking foot attachment for sewing machine

turquoise felt

scraps of blue, green, and yellow gingham

skein of red stranded embroidery floss

6 1 inch (2.5 cm) self-cover buttons

matching sewing thread

sewing kit

sewing machine

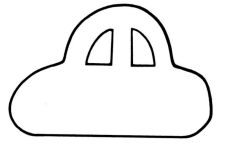

Enlarge templates to 200 percent.

1 Lay the batting flat, place the two pieces of gingham, right sides together, centrally on top of it and smooth them out. Pin, then baste them together around all four edges.

2 Machine-stitch ½ inch (1 cm) from the edge, leaving a 20 inch (50 cm) gap in the center of one edge. Pin and baste under the seam allowance along each side of the gap. Trim the surplus batting and clip the corners.

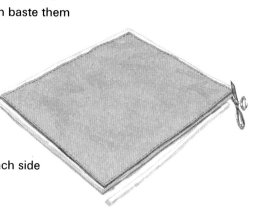

3 Turn right side out through the gap so that the batting is sandwiched between the two pieces of gingham. Close the gap by hand with small slipstitches and press the seams lightly.

4 Use the compass to make two quarter-circle templates from thick tracing paper, with diameters of 7 inches and 7½ inches (17 cm and 19 cm). Enlarge the two heart templates (above) as directed.

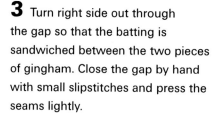

5 Use the chalk pencil and ruler to mark a line 1¼ inches (3 cm) from the four edges. Draw two parallel lines 6 and 7 inches (15 and 18 cm) from each long edge and 7 and 8 inches (18 and 21 cm) from the short edges.

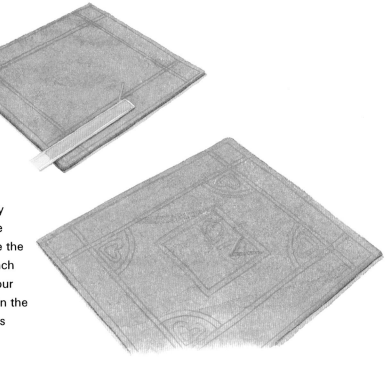

6 Mark two parallel curves at each inside corner by drawing around the quarter-circle templates with the chalk pencil. Draw around the two hearts, one inside the other, within each corner. Measure and mark a 15 inch (38 cm) square in the center of the quilt and draw four double hearts inside. Still using the chalk pencil, fill in the rest of the space with a diamond grid of parallel lines 1¼ inches (3 cm) apart.

7 Starting from the center, baste the three layers together securely by sewing diagonally out to each corner, then to the center of each side. Work parallel lines of basting, approximately 15 cm (6 in) apart, across the whole surface of the quilt.

8 Quilt along all the chalk lines either by hand using quilting thread and a betweens needle or by machine using a special walking foot so that the quilt does not become puckered. If you wish, you can quilt inside the borders with more parallel or wavy lines and add circular motifs to the corners.

9 Cut out three felt cars following the template (opposite). Pin, then baste them in a row along one short edge of the quilt. Sew in place by hand using blanket stitch (see page 105) worked in all six strands of the embroidery thread. Then stitch through just the top layer of fabric.

10 Cover two buttons in each of the three different-colored ginghams and stitch them securely in place to represent the cars' wheels.

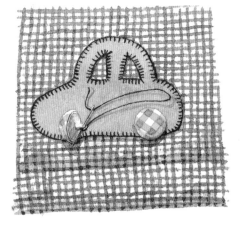

The key to putting together a successful cottage-style bathroom is to get the right combination of informal, traditional good looks and practical, functional modern comfort. You can be imaginative with the basic ingredients, as this is a look that's eclectic and individual—but make sure you avoid furnishings that are too sleek, smart, cool, and sophisticated-looking. For authentic, old-fashioned appeal, you can't beat the capacious luxury of a roll-top bathtub, matched with a generously sized

bathrooms

washbasin. Walls might be covered in tongue and groove, patterned ceramic tiles, or just a wash of colored paint, while the floor might be stone, tile, boards, or linoleum. Make sure that the room is toasty warm with a cast-iron column radiator or a large heated towel rod, and finish with some freestanding storage.

TOP, LEFT *A traditional roll-top bathtub, column radiator, and high-level toilet tank create a sense of timeless style, while the quirky plaster roundel above the tub is charming.*

TOP, RIGHT *The quiet character of this bathroom comes from its mix of soft colors and unassuming furnishings.*

BOTTOM, LEFT *Natural materials are ideal for every room in a country-style house, but particularly so in a bathroom, where you can really appreciate the tactile nature of warm wood, cool stone, and nubby towels.*

BOTTOM, CENTER *Decorated Victorian ceramic tiles make an unusual but effective backsplash next to the tub.*

BOTTOM, RIGHT *Rows of wooden shelves are a good way to store and display bathroom accessories.*

colors & textures

Although white is the standard color for bathroom fixtures, there are plenty of ways in which you can introduce the more interesting shades that characterize country style. Walls might be washed with paint or paneled in natural wood, while the areas next to the bathtub and basin could have jolly hand-painted tiles as a backsplash. Even the floor could be given a few coats of paint, or be covered in patterned ceramic tiles or traditional linoleum. And accessories, from towels to bath oils, can add glorious dashes of color or intriguing surface textures.

In general, watery blues and greens are ideal choices, though a seaside theme including mid-blue, turquoise, primrose yellow, bright red, or bubblegum pink (think of beach cabanas and deckchairs) will also work nicely for this look. Of course, if you want an all-white bathroom, there is nothing wrong with that—provided you include a variety of textures and mix white with naturals, such as wood and wicker, to avoid a sterile, modern effect.

ABOVE, FROM LEFT TO RIGHT *For an all-white bathroom to have the right rustic feel, it's important to include some natural wood and rough, distressed surfaces—such as this beautifully peeling painted floor. Tongue and groove boarding painted a soft, grayish-blue is a traditional choice for a bathroom, especially when combined with a roll-top tub with brass "telephone"-style faucet. Wood-paneled walls are a more down-to-earth alternative to tongue and groove. The lovely warmth of natural wood—in this case, in the form of a sash window and Shaker-style peg rail—contrasts wonderfully with the bright, shiny white of ceramic surfaces.*

LEFT *Here, natural wood has been used for an unpretentious vanity unit, with painted wood for the walls.*

RIGHT *This monochrome scheme is composed mainly of creamy whites, with strong black as an occasional counterpoint.*

LEFT *These sweet gathered curtains are hung from portiere rods on each side of a dormer window. They coordinate nicely with the hand towel and the bath bag that's perched on the shelf above the washbasin. Notice the understated curtain that's been used as a screen below the basin.*

BELOW, FROM LEFT TO RIGHT *The large drying rack rigged up around this roll-top tub functions perfectly as a shower screen, with a couple of ordinary plastic curtains. This half-curtain is ideal for privacy, yet still allows plenty of light through the top half of the window. Wooden blinds are great for larger bathroom windows, and here the whole effect has been softened with the addition of a ruched shade above.*

OPPOSITE *Blue and white checks liven up a plain white bathroom, in the form of a panel strung across the bottom of the window for privacy and a decorative, shaped pelmet at the top.*

fabrics

Fabric doesn't play as large a part in a bathroom as elsewhere in the house, but it can still make a delightful appearance in the form of blinds, neat little curtains, screens across shelving, laundry bags, bathmats, and, of course, towels. What's more, each time you use a length of fabric, it adds a note of softness, fluidity, color, and pattern that combines nicely with the predominantly hard materials elsewhere, such as ceramic and wood. As far as pattern goes, ginghams and other checks are ideal, as are delicate floral patterns, plains or stripes.

When choosing fabrics for window treatments, it's best to concentrate on light cottons, linens, and voiles—nothing too heavy that will retain moisture. You could make them as plain panels with hooks at each end, or gather them over portiere rods or a bamboo pole. Alternatively, a simple roll-up or roman shade, perhaps with a shaped bottom edge, is perfect.

finishing touches

Bathroom furnishings have to be extremely practical, but there are plenty of opportunities to have fun with pretty accessories, too. A nautical theme can be really attractive, with sweet little sailing boats arranged on windowsills or shelves, or beside the bath fixtures. You could also add model lighthouses and beach cabanas, antique ship's fixtures (such as portholes or bulkhead lamps), and naïve maritime paintings. Alternatively, a natural scheme might incorporate shells, pebbles, driftwood, starfish, and sponges. Don't forget storage accessories such as soap dishes and toothbrush holders—they could be made of colored glass, blue-and-white china, or wirework, while freestanding furniture such as rush-seated stools or small, painted cupboards will add to the atmosphere. Mirrors are essential and can easily be embellished to suit your scheme—if you buy one with a plain, broad wooden frame, you could paint it, gild it, or cover it with driftwood, shells, or mosaic tiles. Finally, for a touch of extra color and softness, add a homemade rag rug beside the bathtub and a selection of towels with patterned trimmings.

ABOVE, FROM LEFT TO RIGHT *Soaps don't have to be boring—choose some with pretty colors and shapes, and an irresistible scent, and they become delightful finishing touches. Flowers and foliage cut from the garden can be displayed in an informal container such as a milk bottle or jar. Add a delicately patterned fabric trim to white towels and bathrobes for a really gorgeous country effect.*

OPPOSITE *A row of small books makes for inexpensive storage, while thrift-store finds such as metal buckets or little wooden stools can be put to great use in a country-style bathroom. Here, the owner has casually displayed a small model pond yacht as a decorative touch in what is a really charming, understated, and inexpensive room.*

practicalities

Most of the projects in this book are quick and simple to make by anyone who enjoys kitchen-table craft. Some, however, require a little more expertise and a few pieces of specialist equipment. Even the most challenging, however, should be enjoyable for anyone who is keen and creative. These practical tips should help you on your way.

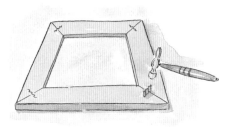

Corrugated fastener

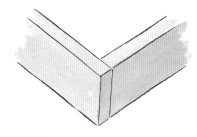

Butt joint

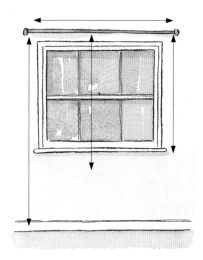

Measuring windows

CORRUGATED FASTENER

Glue the four lengths of wood together to form a flat frame. Clamp the glued corners with miter clamps and reinforce the joints with corrugated fasteners before removing the clamps.

BUTT JOINT

This involves squaring off the ends to be joined, applying glue to one end grain, then lining it up with the side of the other piece. The joint is usually reinforced by pinning through from the back, but corner blocks can be inserted for extra strength.

ADHESIVE

For simplification, when wood glue is specified in the projects, white wood-working glue is meant. Although it is known by many different trade names, it is basically PVA (polyvinyl acetate), a thick water-based adhesive that is transparent when it dries. It is easily applied and sets at room temperature.

Always make sure that the surfaces of wood to be joined fit each other properly and are free from dust. If necessary, smooth them with sandpaper first and then dust them with a soft cloth. Apply enough glue to coat the wood but not so much that it drips and runs—too much glue will weaken the joint. Make sure that the whole surface of the joint is covered with a thin film of glue, then apply pressure by clamping for an hour. If you do not have C-clamps or a suitable vise, then the two pieces can be bound together with taut masking tape until the joint has bonded. PVA is water-resistant but not weatherproof, so it should only be used for interior work if the finished work is not sealed.

SAWING

You should always saw a piece of wood on the waste side of your cutting line. A handsaw should be used to saw your lengths of wood to size before any fine work begins. Mark a cutting line with a soft pencil against a try square, then score along the marked line with a utility knife—this will give the top edge of the wood a smooth finish. Use C-clamps or a vise to secure the wood when making the first few cuts (the idea is to make a channel for the saw blade to follow). Then remove the clamps and, holding the wood near to the blade with your spare hand, gently saw into the wood, keeping the blade lowered and supporting the wood from below for the last strokes. Always make sure your saw is sharp.

MEASURING WINDOWS

Before starting to make curtains, you must first measure the window to calculate how much fabric is needed. This is a very important calculation, so take your time and check your measurements again once you have finished.

If possible, put up the track, pole, or pelmet board in place before measuring the window. The track or pole should be attached 2–6 inches (5–15 cm) above the window frame, with the ends projecting at least 4 inches (10 cm) beyond each side of the window. Take measurements with a metal tape measure, and if the window is very tall or wide get someone to help you.

The two measurements needed to calculate fabric quantities for a pair of curtains are the width and the length of the window. To work out the width of the finished curtains, measure the width of the track, rail, or pole. If you are using a pelmet board, measure the sides and front. To calculate the drop of the finished full-length curtains, measure from the top of the track or bottom of the pole to the floor. For sill-length curtains, measure from the top of the track or bottom of the pole to the sill. For apron-length curtains, measure from the top of the track or pole to just below the sill or to the desired point.

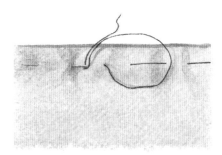

Basting stitch

BASTING STITCH

This temporary stitch is like a larger, looser version of running stitch. It holds fabric in place until it is permanently stitched. Use a colorful thread so the basting is clearly visible and therefore easy to remove.

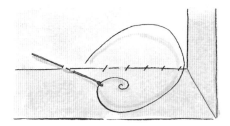

Slipstitch

SLIPSTITCH

Slipstitch holds a folded edge to flat fabric or two folded edges together, as in a mitered corner. Work on the wrong side of the fabric, from right to left. Start with the needle in the fold. Push it out and pick up a few threads from the flat fabric, then insert it into the hem again, all in one smooth and continuous movement. When finished, the stitches should be almost invisible.

BLANKET STITCH

A decorative stitch for finishing edges. Secure the thread at one end of the fabric, and working from right to left, insert the needle about ½ inch (1 cm) from the edge; keep the thread under the point of the needle and complete the stitch to create a loop. Continue to work the stitches every ½ inch (1 cm) or so, making sure the height is even.

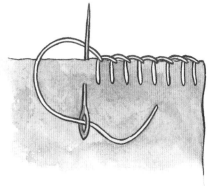

Blanket stitch

MITERING CORNERS

Mitering is the neatest way of working hem corners. Press in the hem allowance along the bottom and sides of the fabric; then open it out flat again. Where the two fold lines meet, turn in the corner of the fabric diagonally. Turn in the hems along the pressed fold to form a neat diagonal line. Use slipstitch to secure.

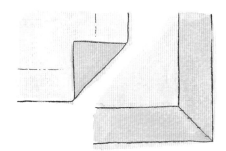

Mitering corners

MAKING TIES AND TABS

To make a tie, cut a strip of material to the desired width and length. Fold the strip in half along the length, wrong sides together, and press. Pin, baste, and machine-sew all along the long side and one short end, leaving the other short end unstitched. Push the tie right side out with the aid of a knitting needle. Turn in a ¼ inch (5 mm) fold to the inside of the tie, press in place and slipstitch the end closed. Tabs are made in exactly the same way as ties—the only difference is that the strip of fabric is wider and they are usually buttoned, not tied.

Making ties and tabs

sources

ABC Carpet & Home
888 Broadway
New York, NY 10003
t. 212-473-3000
www.abccarpet.com
Large-scale home accessories store, specializing in carpets.

Bed, Bath, & Beyond
620 Avenue of the Americas
New York, NY 10011
t. 212-255-3550
www.bedbathandbeyond.com
Department stores with everything for the home.

Blanks Fabrics
6709 Whitestone Road
Baltimore, MD 21207
t. 410-944-0040
www.blanksfab.com
Will track down those hard to find fabrics and textiles from around the world.

Calico Fabric Shop
10 West Street
W. Hatfield, MA 01088–954
t. 413-247-9989
www.calicofabric.com
Largest quilt shop in central and western Massachusetts. Inventory includes all major fabric manufacturing companies. Online catalog available.

Cape Cod Crafters
Route 1
Freeport, ME 04032
t. 207-865-1691
www.capecodcrafters.com
Ribbons, candles, and table decorations.

Carolina Candle Co.
6831 US Highway 311
Sophia, NC 27350
t. 336-498-5786
www.carolinacandlecompany.com
A nearly limitless collection of tapers, votives, tea lights, and pillars is available here, as are various aromatherapy candles.

Cath Kidston
201 Mulberry Street
New York, NY 10012
t. 212-343-0223
www.cathkidston.com
Bright and fresh 1950s-inspired florals and accessories. Fabrics available.

Conso Products
P.O. Box 326
Union, SC 29379
t. 800-842-6676
www.conso.com
One of the largest distributors of decorative trims, cording, ropings, tassels, and fringes in various fibers.

Covington Candle
976 Lexington Avenue
New York, NY 10021
t. 212-472-1131
Tapers in 30 colors and six sizes, which will fit perfectly into different holders and decors. Pillars are also available in a number of sizes to order.

Crate & Barrel
646 N Michigan Avenue
Chicago, IL 60611
t. 312-787-5900
www.crateandbarrel.com
A wonderful source of good-value china, glass, and plastic containers. Locations nationwide. Mail order. Catalog.

Fabrics To Dye For
1 Charlestown Beach Road
Charlestown, RI 02813
www.fabricstodyefor.com
Large selection of hand-painted fabrics and yarns, surface design art supplies, and weaving supplies.

FloraCraft
One Longfellow Place
P.O.Box 400
Ludington, MI 49431
t. 231-845-5127
f. 231-845-0240
www.floracraft.com
Distributors of wreath, topiary, and geometric forms made of Styrofoam, extruded foam, and straw; also available is a vast array of floral supplies and accessories.

Fiskars Manufacturing Corp.
P.O. Box 1727
Wausau, WI 54401
t. 715-842-2091
www.fiskars.com
Manufacturers of fine-quality scissors, snippers, paper edgers, and punchers, and the useful Craft-Snip, which can be used to cut a variety of heavy-duty materials. They also make excellent tools for gardening and floral work.

Hancock Fabrics
2605A West Main Street
Tupelo, MS 38801
t. 662-844-7368
www.hancockfabrics.com
Everything you need for projects involving sewing or fabrics, including adhesives.

High Country Floral
P.O. Box 155
Carlton, WA 98814
t. 509-923-2646
f. 509-923-2037
www.highcountryfloral.com
Here you can find preserved and stem-dyed wreaths, garlands, and arches, as well as a wide selection of other preserved and dried flowers and leaves, herbs, and spices.

Hobby Lobby
t. 405-745-1100; ask for Customer Service
www.hobbylobby.com
Discount arts and crafts stores. Locations nationwide.

Hollywood Trims
A division of Prym-Dritz Corp.
P.O. Box 5028
Spartanburg, SC 29304
t. 800-255-7796
www.dritz.com
Rayon, cotton, and metallic trims, cordings, and tassels.

Home Depot
t. 800-553-3199
www.homedepot.com
A wide selection of lumber, outdoor furniture, and plant material at discounted prices.

Ikea
www.ikea.com
Affordable home accessories, vases and paper products. Locations nationwide.

Jo-Ann Stores, Inc.
13323 Riverside Drive
Sherman Oaks, CA 91423-2508
t. 818-789-3167
t. 800-525-4951 for enquiries
www.joann.com
Craft supplies for all projects. Locations nationwide.

Kate's Paperie
561 Broadway
New York, NY 10012
t. 212-941-9816
Over 40,000 papers, many handmade, plus cards, journals, and wrappings.

Lion Ribbon Company, Inc.
An affiliate of C.M. Offray & Son
Route 24, P.O. Box 601
Chester, NJ 07930
t. 800-344-5533
www.offray.com
Craft and specialty ribbons, including burlap and wired kinds, in a broad selection of colors, fabrics, and widths. Widely available in craft and variety stores, as well as floral supply shops.

Loose Ends
P.O. Box 20310
Keizer, OR 97307
t. 503-390-7457
www.looseends.com
A wide selection of natural-fiber papers, ribbons, and botanicals, like seagrass, raffia, dried fruits, and fungi.

Lowe's
www.lowes.com
Locations nationwide.
Good source of garden accessories, tools, and lumber.

Maple Ridge Supply
9528 South Bolton Road
Posen, MI 49776
t. 517-356-4807
f. 517-354-6664
www.mapleridgesupply.com
All sizes and shapes of metal wreath forms.

May Silk
16202 Distribution Way
Cerritos, CA 90703
t. 562-926-1818
A complete line of silk flowers, plants, foliage, trees, arangements, and floral accessories is available here.

Melinamade Fabrics
420 Russell Street
Winters, CA 95694
t. 415-902-8460
www.melinamade.com
Vintage inspired patterns on Barkcloth cotton fabrics, wallpaper, and accessories.

Michaels Stores, Inc.
t. 800-MICHAELS for a store near you
www.michaels.com
Specialty retailer of arts and crafts items. Locations nationwide.

M & J Trim
1008 Sixth Avenue
New York, NY 10018
t. 212-842-5000
www.mjtrim.com
Has an outstanding collection of decoorative trims, cording, ropings, tassels, and fringes in various fibers.

M.P.R. Associates, Inc.
P.O. Box 7343
High Point, NC 27264
t. 800-454-3331
This maker of nontraditional ribbons can provide you with paper lace, corrugated paper ribbons, wired and plain paper and metallic ribbons, paper raffia, and paper twist.

A. C. Moore
Styretowne Plaza
1069 Bloomfield Ave
Clifton, NJ 07012
t. 973-470-8885
www.acmoore.com
Craft superstores. Over 70 stores throughout Eastern US.

Nature's Holler
15739 Old Lowery Road North
Omaha, AR 72662
t. 870-426-5489
Everything for dried arrangements; grapevine wreaths, acorns, pods, pine cones, weeds and grasses, moss, bamboo, and wood works.

Northern Lights Candles
3474 Andover Road
Wellsville, NY 14895
t. 800-836-8797
www.northernlightscandles.com
Candles of all varieties are available here, from scented to columns of geometric forms; also molded novelty and made-to-drip specialty candles.

On Board Fabrics
Route 27
P.O. Box 14
Edgecomb, ME 04556
t. 207-882-7536
www.onboardfabrics.com
Offering a large selection of decorating fabrics, including woven plaids, Italian tapestries, and Balinese cottons.

Pier One Imports
71 Fifth Avenue
New York, NY 10003
t. 212-206-1911
www.pier1.com
A specialty retailer offering furniture and home accessories with a distinctive international flavor.

PJ's Decorative Fabrics, Inc.
511 West Broad Avenue
Albany, GA 31701
t. 229-439-7265
www.pjsfabrics.com
Carries a large selection of home decorating fabrics, trims, rugs, and more.

Pottery Barn
600 Broadway
New York, NY 10012
t. 212-219-2420
www.potterybarn.com
Moderately priced garden furniture, a variety of glassware, candlesticks, and hurricane lamps. Locations nationwide.

Rag Shops, Inc.
t. 973-423-1303; ask for Customer Service
www.ragshop.com
Offering a wide selection of value-priced crafts, fabrics, floral, framing, and related merchandise for the crafter and home sewer.

Robert Allen
www.robertallendesign.com
Quality decorative fabrics. Nationwide storerooms.

Scalamandre Fabrics
222 East 59th Street
New York, NY 10022
t. 212-980-3888
www.scalamandre.com
Luxury textile manufacturer.

Smith and Hawken
2 Arbor Lane
P.O. Box 6900
Florence, KY 41022-6900
t. 800-776-3336
www.smith-hawken.com
Wide variety of ornaments, plants, tools, and furniture, Locations nationwide. Mail order. Catalog.

Stonemountain & Daughter Fabrics
2518 Shattuck Avenue
Berkeley, CA 94704
t. 510-845-6106
www.stonemountainfabric.com
A full service, old-fashioned fabric store. All-natural fabrics are their specialty. They also carry an extensive collection of unique buttons, patterns, and notions.

Sunshine Drapery Company
11660 Page Service Drive
St. Louis, MO 63146
t. 314-569-2980
www.sunshinedrapery.com
Thousands of in-stock fabrics and trim of every style.

Tinsel Trading Co.
47 West 38th Street
New York, NY 10018
t. 212-730-1030
www.tinseltrading.com
Unique vintage-to-contemporary trims, tassels, fringes, and cords.

The Ribbonerie
191 Potrero Avenue
San Francisco, CA 94103
t. 415-626-6184
www.theribbonerie.com
Specialty ribbon store, featuring ribbons from around the world.

Tom Thumb Workshops
59 Market Street
Onocock VA 23417
t. 800-526-6502
Craft products, dried and pressed flowers, and skeletonized leaves can be found here, as well as potpourri, herbs, spices, and essential oils.

Wal-Mart
t. 501-273-4000
www.walmart.com
Locations nationwide.

Waverly Home Store
For stores and stockists visit:
www.waverly.com

Walnut Hollow
1409 State Road 23
Dodgeville, WI 53533
t. 800-395-5995
Manufactures just about any unfinished wooden shape imagineable, from birdhouses to candle cups.

Westgate Fabrics
905 Avenue T
Suite 905
Grand Prairie, TX 75053
t. 800-527-2517
www.westgatefabrics.com
Great range of fabrics and trimmings.

Wood-N-Crafts, Inc.
P.O. Box 140
Lakeview, MI 48850
t. 800-444-8075
f. 517-352-6792
www.wood-n-crafts.com
A good source for unfinished wood, such as candlesticks and candle cups, buttons, stars, and hearts.

picture credits

Key: *ph= photographer, il= illustrator, a=above, b=below, r=right, l=left, c=center.*

Endpapers ph Christopher Drake; 1 ph Christopher Drake/refurbishment and interior design by Chichi Meroni Fassio, Parnassus; 2 Polly Eltes/Sheila Scholes' house near Cambridge; 3 ph James Merrell/Hotel de la Mirande; 4al & br ph Simon Upton; 4c ph Caroline Arber; 5 ph Catherine Gratwicke/designer Caroline Zoob's home in East Sussex; 7 ph Simon Upton; 9 ph James Merrell; 10al ph Alan Williams/the Norfolk home of Geoff and Gilly Newberry of Bennison Fabrics–on walls: Tulip Tree in pink and green on beige linen by Bennison; 10–11a ph Alan Williams/Louise Robbins' house in North West Herefordshire; 10bl ph Jan Baldwin/Mark Smith's home in the Cotswolds; 10br ph Chris Everard/a house in London designed by Helen Ellery of The Plot London, paintings by Robert Clarke; 11ar ph Alan Williams/the Norfolk home of Geoff and Gilly Newberry of Bennison Fabrics–on walls: Daisy Chain on oyster linen; 11bl ph Tom Leighton/Marilyn Phipps' house in Kent; 12al ph Simon Upton; 12ac ph James Merrell/Mary Drysdale; 12–13a ph Simon Upton/the home of Julia and Glen Vague, Kentucky, designed by Jacomini Interior Design; 12–13b ph Simon Upton/the Jacomini Family Farm, designed by Jacomini Interior Design; 13a ph Simon Upton/Mrs Robin Elverson's house near Round Top, Texas; 13b ph James Merrell; 14a ph Christopher Drake/Alain and Catherine Brunel's home and hotel, La Maison Douce, Saint-Martin de Ré; 14bl ph Tom Leighton; 14br ph Simon Upton; 15a both ph Christopher Drake/Florence and Pierre Pallardy, Domaine de la Baronnie, St-Martin de Ré; 16al & ac ph Polly Wreford/Lena Proudlock's home Gloucestershire has since been restyled; 16–17a & 16–17b ph Simon Upton/Lena Proudlock's home Gloucestershire has since been restyled; 17ac ph Christopher Drake/Nordic Style Bedroom; 17ar ph Simon Upton/Lena Proudlock's home Gloucestershire has since been restyled; 17br ph James Merrell; 19 ph David Montgomery/Sheila Scholes' house near Cambridge; 20al ph Christopher Drake/Julie Prisca's house in Normandy; 20bl ph James Merrell; 20ac & 20–21a ph Simon Upton/the home of Julia and Glen Vague, Kentucky, designed by Jacomini Interior Design; 20c & 20–21b ph Simon Upton; 22al & bl ph Christopher Drake/owners of La Cour Beaudeval Antiquities, Mireille and Jean Claude Lothon's house in Faverolles; 22ar ph Polly Wreford/Mary Foley's house in Connecticut; 23a ph Alan Williams/the Norfolk home of Geoff and Gilly Newberry of Bennison Fabrics- on walls: Chinese pheasant on oatmeal linen by Bennison; 23b ph Christopher Drake/Lee Freund's Summerhouse in Southampton, New York; 24l ph Alan Williams/the Arbuthnott family's house near Cirencester designed by Nicholas Arbuthnott, fabrics designed by Vanessa Arbuthnott; 24c ph Tom Leighton; 24–25 ph Alan Williams/Miv Watts' house in Norfolk; 26 ph David Montgomery, 26–27 il Michael Hill; 28al ph Polly Wreford/The Sawmills Studios; 28bl ph Christopher Drake/Florence and Pierre Pallardy, Domaine de la Baronnie, St-Martin de Ré; 28ac ph James Merrell/cushions from The Blue Door; 28ar ph Christopher Drake/owner Monique Davidson's family home in Normandy; 28cr ph Catherine Gratwicke/interior designer Sue West's house in Gloucestershire-selection of cushions on sofa made by Sue West; 28br ph David Montgomery/Sasha Waddell's house in London; 29l ph James Merrell; 29r ph Debi Treloar/Mark and Sally of Baileys Home & Garden's house in Herefordshire; 30a ph Catherine Gratwicke/interior designer Sue West's house in Gloucestershire—blind made from tea-towel-style fabric from The Housemade; 30b ph Catherine Gratwicke/designer Caroline Zoob's home in East Sussex—selection of cushions made from antique fabric by Caroline Zoob, blind made from antique linen; 30–31 ph Polly Eltes/blind design by Sian and Annie Colley; 32ph James Merrell/fabrics from Sandersons, ties from John Lewis; 32–33 il Jacqueline Pestell; 34al ph Jan Baldwin/the owner of Tessuti, Catherine Vindevogel-Debal's house in Kortrijk, Belgium; 34bl ph Caroline Arber/Linda Garman's home in London; 34bc ph Henry Bourne; 34br ph Caroline Arber; 35 ph Caroline Arber/Linda Garman's home in London; 36l ph James Merrell; 36r ph Chris Everard/a house in London designed by Helen Ellery of The Plot London; 37a ph Christopher Drake/Josephine Ryan's house in London; 37bl & br ph James Merrell; 37bc ph David Montgomery; 38 ph James Merrell; 38–39 il Lizzie Sanders; 40 ph James Merrell; 40–41 il Helen Smythe; 42al ph David Montgomery/a house in Connecticut designed by Lynn Morgan Design; 42bl ph David Montgomery/Sasha Waddell's house in

London; 42–43a ph Simon Upton; 42br ph Henry Bourne; 43b ph James Merrell; 44al ph Simon Upton; 44–45 James Merrell; 45ar ph Simon Upton/Lena Proudlock's home Gloucestershire has since been restyled; 45br ph Christopher Drake/owners of La Cour Beaudeval Antiquities, Mireille and Jean Claude Lothon's house in Faverolles; 46al ph James Merrell; 46ar & 47 ph James Merrell/Mary Drysdale; 48al ph Catherine Gratwicke/owner of Adamczewski, Hélène Adamczewski's house in Lewes—antique patchwork quilt from Grace & Favour; 48cl & bl ph David Montgomery/Sasha Waddell's house in London; 48–49a ph Henry Bourne; 48–49b ph Christopher Drake/owners of La Cour Beaudeval Antiquities, Mireille and Jean Claude Lothon's house in Faverolles; 49 ph David Montgomery; 50al ph David Montgomery/a house in Connecticut designed by Lynn Morgan Design; 50ar ph Christopher Drake/Nordic Style; 50br ph Simon Upton/a residence in Highlands, North Carolina, designed by Nancy Braithwaite Interiors; 51al ph Henry Bourne; 51ar ph Simon Upton; 51b ph James Merrell; 52 ph Christopher Drake/Mr and Mrs Degrugillier, Le Mas de Flore, Antiquite et Creation, Lagnes, Isle sur Sorgue, Provence; patchwork tablecloth, tea service and plates, L'Utile e il Dilettevole; 52–53 il Lizzie Sanders; 54al ph Christopher Drake/Lincoln Cato's house in Brighton; 54ar ph Henry Bourne; 54b both Polly Wreford; 55b ph Catherine Gratwicke/the home of Patty Collister in London, owner of An Angel At My Table–jug cover from the Dining Room Shop, place mats from Tobias & The Angel; 55a ph Caroline Arber/Linda Garman's home in London; 56 ph James Merrell; 56–57 il Lizzie Sanders; 58al ph Andrew Wood; 58bl ph James Merrell/Baron and Baroness de Mitri de Gunzburg's house in Provence; 58–59a ph James Merrell/Janick and Hubert Schoumacher-Vilfroy's house in Normandy; 59c ph Christopher Drake/interior designer Carole Oulhen; 59b ph David Montgomery/Sheila Scholes' house near Cambridge; 60al ph James Merrell/Mr and Mrs Barrow's house in Surrey designed by architects Marshall Haines and Barrow/kitchen by Chalon; 60–61a ph James Merrell/Vicky and Simon Young's house in Northumberland; 61b ph Simon Upton/Conner Prairie open-air living museum; 61a ph Alan Williams/Louise Robbins' house in northwest Herefordshire; 62al ph Tom Leighton/paint Farrow & Ball: floor Mouse's Back floor paint no. 40, cupboards Green Smoke no. 47 and interior Red Fox no. 48, walls and woodwork String no. 8, ceiling Off White no. 3; 62ar ph James Merrell; 62b ph Polly Wreford/Story; 63a ph Christopher Drake/Florence and Pierre Pallardy, Domaine de la Baronnie, St-Martin de Ré; 63b ph Andrew Wood; 64 ph David Montgomery; 64–65 il Michael Hill; 66al ph James Merrell; 66bl ph Simon Upton; 66ar ph Caroline Arber; 66cr & 67a ph Catherine Gratwicke/designer Caroline Zoob's home in East Sussex—patchwork curtains made by Caroline Zoob from antique fabric; 66br & 67bl ph Catherine Gratwicke/owner of Adamczewski, Hélène Adamczewski's house in Lewes—antique ticking on table and in cupboard from Kim Sully Antiques, all ceramics from Adamczewski; 67br ph Christopher Drake/Ali Sharland's former home in Gloucestershire; 68l ph James Merrell; 68r ph Simon Upton/Plain English; 69a & 69bl ph Catherine Gratwicke/interior designer Sue West's house in Gloucestershire—linen covered notebooks and napkin box with initial from The Housemade; 69bc ph Polly Wreford/Linda Garman's home in London, patchwork tablecloth by Rob Merrett; 69br ph Catherine Gratwicke/Claudia Bryant's house in London—glove from Grace & Favour, lined with Liberty print fabric; 70 ph James Merrell; 70–71 il Michael Hill; 72a ph Simon Upton/Plain English; 72bl ph Tom Leighton; 72br ph Henry Bourne; 73al ph Christopher Drake/Annie-Camille Kuentzmann-Levet's house in the Yvelines; 73ar ph Christopher Drake/owner Monique Davidson's family home in Normandy; 73b ph Simon Upton; 74 ph Christopher Drake/Lincoln Cato's house in Brighton; 75a & bl ph Simon Upton/Plain English; 75bc ph Simon Upton; 75br ph Caroline Arber; 76 ph David Montgomery; 76–77 il Michael Hill; 78al ph James Merrell/Hotel Villa Gallici; 78ac & c ph Christopher Drake/Ali Sharland's former home in Gloucestershire; 78bl ph Jan Baldwin/Michael D'Souza of Mufti; 78–79a ph Tom Leighton/Fay and Roger Oates' house in Ledbury; 78–79b ph Jan Baldwin/a house in Maine designed by Stephen Blatt Architects; 80a ph Tom Leighton; 80b ph Christopher Drake/Warner Johnson's apartment in New York designed by Edward Cabot of Cabot Design Ltd.; 80–81 ph Tom Leighton; 81a ph Alan Williams/the Arbuthnott family's house near Cirencester designed by Nicholas Arbuthnott, fabrics designed by Vanessa Arbuthnott; 81b ph Alan Williams/Louise Robbins' house in northwest Herefordshire; 82al ph Chris Everard/a house in London designed by Helen Ellery of The Plot London, paintings by Robert Clarke; 82bl ph Tom Leighton; 82ar ph Ray Main/Marina and Peter Hill's barn in West Sussex designed by Marina Hill, Peter James Construction Management, Chichester, The West Sussex Antique

Timber Company, Wisborough Green, and Joanna Jefferson Architects; **83al** ph Christopher Drake/Alain and Catherine Brunel's home and hotel, La Maison Douce, Saint-Martin de Ré; **83ar** ph James Merrell; **83b** ph James Merrell/architect, Jim Ruscitto; **84** ph James Merrell; **84–85** il Helen Smythe; **86a** ph Catherine Gratwicke/designer Caroline Zoob's home in East Sussex—lampshade an original design by Caroline Zoob; **86c** ph Henry Bourne; **86b** Nelly Guyot's house in Ramatuelle, France, styled by Nelly Guyot; **87l** ph David Montgomery/Sasha Waddell's house in London; **87c** ph Catherine Gratwicke/Rose Hammick's home in London—covered box from Braemar Antiques, button bag from An Angel At My Table; **87b** ph Christopher Drake/owners of French Country Living, the Hill family's home on the Côte d'Azur; **87ar** ph Debi Treloar; **88a** ph James Merrell; **88bl** ph Catherine Gratwicke; **88bc** ph Christopher Drake/owners of La Cour Beaudeval Antiquities, Mireille and Jean Claude Lothon's house in Faverolles; **88br** ph Catherine Gratwicke; **89al** ph Christopher Drake/owner Monique Davidson's family home in Normandy; **89ar** ph Christopher Drake/Annie-Camille Kuentzmann-Levet's house in the Yvelines; **90** ph Catherine Gratwicke/Rose Hammick's home in London, quilt made by Lucinda Ganderton; **90–91** il Lizzie Sanders; **92al, ar & br** ph James Merrell; **92cr** ph Christopher Drake/Tita Bay's village house in Ramatuelle; **92bl** ph Caroline Arber; **93a** ph Christopher Drake/Alain and Catherine Brunel's home and hotel, La Maison Douce, Saint-Martin de Ré; **93b** ph Jan Baldwin/Roderick and Gillie James' house in Devon designed by Roderick James Architects and built by Carpenter Oak & Woodland Co. Ltd.; **94** ph Sandra Lane; **94–95** il Lizzie Sanders; **96al** ph Chris Everard/Emma & Neil's house in London, walls painted by Garth Carter; **96bl** ph Christopher Drake/Eva Johnson's house in Suffolk, interiors designed by Eva Johnson; **96–97a** ph Christopher Drake/interior designer Carole Oulhen; **96–97b** ph Christopher Drake/Enrica Stabile's house in Le Thor, Provence; **97b** ph Simon Upton/a residence in Highlands, North Carolina, designed by Nancy Braithwaite Interiors; **98al** ph Christopher Drake/owner Monique Davidson's family home in Normandy; **98ar** ph Jan Baldwin/a house in Maine designed by Stephen Blatt Architects; **98b** ph Simon Upton/a residence in Highlands, North Carolina, designed by Nancy Braithwaite Interiors; **99al** ph Ray Main/Marina and Peter Hill's barn in West Sussex designed by Marina Hill, Peter James Construction Management, Chichester, The West Sussex Antique Timber Company, Wisborough Green, and Joanna Jefferson Architects; **99ar** ph James Merrell; **99b** ph Christopher Drake/Eva Johnson's house in Suffolk, interiors designed by Eva Johnson; **100a** ph Catherine Gratwicke/designer Caroline Zoob's home in East Sussex—floral Dorothy bag made by Caroline Zoob; **100bl** ph Henry Bourne/Fay and Roger Oates' house in Ledbury; **100bc** ph James Merrell; **100br** Simon Upton/a residence in Highlands, North Carolina, designed by Nancy Braithwaite Interiors; **101** ph James Merrell; **102l** ph Christopher Drake/Enrica Stabile's house in Brunello; **102c** ph James Merrell; **102r** ph Catherine Gratwicke/interior designer Sue West's house in Gloucestershire—pink mug and toile-edged towels from Grace & Favour; **103** ph James Merrell; **104, 105ac & 105bc** il Michael Hill; **105a & b** il Lizzie Sanders; **105c** il Jacqueline Pestell.

Architects and designers whose work is featured in this book

Adamczewski
fine houseware
88 High Street
Lewes
East Sussex, BN7 1XN
UK
t. +44 1273 470105
adamczewski@onetel.net.uk
pages 48al, 66br, 67bl

An Angel At My Table
t. +44 20 7424 9777
www.angelatmytable.co.uk
pages 55b, 87c

Annie-Camille Kuentzmann-Levet
Décoration
3 Ter, Rue Mathieu Le Coz
La Noue
78980 Mondreville
France
t./f. +33 1 30 42 53 59
pages 73al, 89ar

Arne Maynard Garden Design
71 New Kings Road
London, SW6 4SQ
UK
pages 24c, 80–81a

Baileys Home & Garden
The Engine Shed
Station Approach
Ross-on-Wye
Herefordshire, HR9 7BW
UK
t. +44 1989 563015
f. +44 1989 768172
sales@baileys-home-garden.co.uk
www.baileyshomeandgarden.com
page 29r

Bennison Fabrics
16 Holbein Place
London, SW1W 8NL
UK
t. +44 20 7730 8076
f. +44 20 7823 4997
bennisonfabrics@btinternet.com
www.bennisonfabrics.com
pages 10al, 11ar, 23a

Cabot Design Ltd.
interior design
1925 Seventh Avenue, Suite 71
New York, NY 10026
t. 212 222 9488
eocabot@aol.com
page 80b

Carole Oulhen
interior designer
t. +33 6 80 99 66 16
f. +33 4 90 02 01 91
pages 59c, 96–97a

Caroline Zoob
Shop A
33 Cliffe High Street
Lewes
East Sussex, BN7 2AN
UK
t. +44 1273 476464
(shop & mail order)
www.carolinezoob.com
hand-made collectables
pages 5, 30b, 66cr, 67a, 86a, 100a

Carpenter Oak Ltd.
The Framing Yard
East Cornworthy
Totnes
Devon, TQ9 7HF
UK
t. +44 1803 732900
www.carpenteroak.com
page 93b

Conner Prairie
open-air living history museum
13400 Allisonville Road
Fishers, IN 46038
t. 800 966 1836
www.connerprairie.org
page 61b

Claudia Bryant
t. +44 20 7602 2852
page 69br

Domaine de la Baronnie
21 Rue Baron de Chantal
17410 Saint-Martin-de-Ré
France
t. +33 5 46 09 21 29
f. +33 5 46 09 95 29
info@domainedelabaronnie.com
www.domainedelabaronnie.com
pages 15a both, 28bl, 63a

Enrica Stabile
antiques dealer, interior decorator
and photographic stylist
L'Utile e il Dilettevole
Via Carlo Maria Maggi 6
20154 Milano
Italy
t. +39 0234 53 60 86
www.enricastabile.com
pages 52–53, 96–97b, 102l

Eva Johnson
interior designer
t. +44 1638 731 362
f. +44 1638 731 855
www.evajohnson.com
distributor of TRIP TRAP wood
floor treatment products
pages 96bl, 99b

Farrow & Ball
Uddens Estate
Wimborne
Dorset, BH21 7NL
UK
t. +44 1202 876141
f. +44 1202 873793
www.farrowandball.com
page 62al

French Country Living
antiques and decoration
21 Rue De L'Eglise
06250 Mougins
France
t. +33 4 93 75 53 03
f. +33 4 93 75 63 03
f.c.l.com@wanadoo.fr
page 87b

Garth Carter
t. +44 7958 412953
page 96al

Helen Ellery
The Plot London
interior design
77 Compton Street
London, EC1V 0BN
UK
t. +44 20 7251 8116
f. +44 20 7251 8117
helen@theplotlondon.com
www.theplotlondon.com
pages 10br, 36r, 82al

Hotel de la Mirande
Avignon
France
page 3

Hotel Villa Gallici
Aix-en-Provence
France
page 78al

J&M Davidson
Gallery;
97 Golborne Road
London W10 5NL
Shop;
42 Ledbury Road
London W11 2SE
UK
pages 28ar, 73ar, 89al, 98al

Jacomini Interior Design
1701 Brun Street, Suite 101
Houston TX 77019
t. 713 524 8224
f. 713 524 0951
www.jacominidesign.com
*pages 12-13a, 12-13b, 20ac,
20-21a*

Jim Ruscitto, Architect
Ruscitto, Latham, Blanton
PO Box 419
Sun Valley Idaho
ID 83353
f. 208 726 1033
page 83b

Joanna Jefferson Architects
222 Oving Road
Chichester
West Sussex PO19 4EJ
UK
t. +44 1243 532398
f. +44 1243 531550
jjeffearch@aol.com
pages 82ar, 99al

Josephine Ryan
antiques and interiors
63 Abbeville Road
London SW4 9JW
UK
t. +44 20 8675 3900
page 37a

Julie Prisca
46 Rue du Bac
75007 Paris
France
t. +33 1 45 48 13 29
infos@julieprisca.com
www.julieprisca.com
page 20al

La Maison Douce
25 rue Mérindot
17410 St-Martin-de-Ré
France
t. +33 546 09 20 20
t. +33 546 09 09 90
www.lamaisondouce.com
pages 14a, 83al, 93a

Lena Proudlock
www.lenaproudlock.com
*pages 16, 16-17a, 16-17b,
17ar, 45ar*

Lincoln Cato
t. +44 1273 325334
pages 54al, 74
Louise Robbins
Insideout House and Garden
Agency and Malt House
Bed & Breakfast
Malt House, Almeley,
Herefordshire, HR3 6PY
UK
t. +44 1544 340681
lulawrence1@aol.com
www.insideout
-house&garden.co.uk
pages 10-11a, 61a, 81b

Lynn Morgan Design
118 Goodwives River Road
Darien, CT 06820
pages 42al, 50l

Mark Smith at Smithcreative
15 St Georges Road
London, W4 1AU
UK
t. +44 20 8747 3909
f. +44 20 8742 3902
mark@smithcreative.net
ceramics by David Garland
t. 01285 720307
page 10bl

Marshall Haines and Barrow
Gresham House
24 Holburn Viaduct
London EC1A 2BN
UK
t. +44 20 7248 6622
www.mhbdesigngroup.com
page 60al

Mary Drysdale
Drysdale, Inc
78 Kalorama Cir NW
Washington DC 20008
t. 202 588 0700
pages 12ac, 46ar, 47

Mireille and Jean Claude Lothon
La Cour Beaudeval Antiquities
4 rue des Fontaines
28210 Faverolles
France
t. +33 2 37 51 47 67
*pages 22al, 22bl, 45br, 48-49b,
88bc*

Miv Watts Design
House Bait I
t. +44 1328 730557
House Bait II
t. +44 1328 730583
www.wattswishedfor.com
pages 24-25
Mufti
789 Fulham Road
London SW6 5HA
UK
t. +44 20 7610 9123
f. +44 20 7384 2050
www.mufti.co.uk
pages 78bl

Nancy Braithwaite Interiors
2300 Peachtree Road
Suite C101
Atlanta, GA 30309
t. 404 355 1740
f. 404 355 8693
pages 50br, 97b, 98b, 101br

Nelly Guyot
Décoratrice
t. +33 6 09 25 20 68
page 86b

Nordic Style
Classic Swedish Interiors
109 Lots Road
London SW10 0RN
UK
t. +44 20 7351 1755
www.nordicstyle.com
pages 17ac, 50ar

Parnassus
corso Porta Vittoria, 5
Milan
Italy
t. +39 02 78 11 07
page 1

Peter Hone
garden antique consultant,
appointments only
5 Ladbroke Square
London W11 3LX
UK
page 82bl

Plain English
cupboardmakers
Stowupland Hall
Stowupland
Stowmarket
Suffolk IP14 4BE
UK
t. +44 1449 774028
www.plainenglishdesign.com
page 68r, 72a, 75a, 75bl

Roderick James Architects
Seagull House
Dittisham Mill Creek
Dartmouth
Devon TQ6 0HZ
UK
t. +44 1803 722474
www.roderickjamesarchitects.com
page 93b

Roger Oates
London Showroom
1 Munro Terrace (off Riley Street)
London SW10 0DL
UK
t. +44 20 7351 2288
Eastnor Shop
The Long Barn, Eastnor
Herefordshire HR8 1EL
UK
t. +44 1531 631611
www.rogeroates.co.uk
pages 78-79a, 100bl

Sasha Waddell
269 Wandsworth Bridge Road
London SW6 2TX
UK
t. +44 20 7736 0766
pages 28br, 42bl, 48cl, 48bl, 87l

Sharland & Lewis
52 Long Street
Tetbury
Gloucester GL8 8AQ
UK
t. +44 1666 500354
www.sharlandandlewis.com
pages 67br, 78ac, 78c

Sheila Scholes
designer
t. +44 1480 498241
pages 2, 19, 59b

Sian Colley Soft Furnishings
Block E 2B Upper Ringway
Bounds Green
London N11 2UD
UK
t./f. +44 20 8368 4092
colleysian@hotmail.com
pages 30-31

Stephen Blatt Architects
10 Danforth Street
Portland
Maine 04112-0583
t. 207 761 5911
www.sbarchitects.com
pages 78-79b, 98ar

Story
4 Wilkes Street
London E1 6QF
UK
t. +44 20 7377 0313
page 62b

Sue West
The Housemade
interior & product design
t./f. +44 1453 757771
sue.west@btopenworld.com
www.avaweb.co.uk/coachhouse.html
pages 28cr, 30a, 69a, 69bl, 102r

Tessuti
interiors & fabrics
Doorniksewijk 76, 8500 Kortrijk
Belgium
t. +32 56 25 29 27
info@tessuti.be
www.tessuti.be
page 34al

Tita Bay
interior decorator
via Sudorno, 22D
24100 Bergamo
Italy
t. +39 03 52 58 384
page 92cr

Vanessa Arbuthnott Fabrics
www.vanessaarbuthnott.co.uk
holiday lets: www.thetallet.co.uk
pages 24l, 81a

index

acknowledgments

With thanks to Miriam for making the writing process so pleasant and easy. And with love to my wonderful family—especially Martin, Felix, and Tegan.